# CONTENTS

Acknowledgments ➤ 6
Introduction ➤ 6
**Things to Know About Paddling on Georgian Bay** ➤ 9

**Section 1**
    The North Shore 1.0 ➤ **13**
    The Foxes 1.1 ➤ **15**
    Phillip Edward Island 1.2 ➤ **19**
    Killarney to Key River 1.3 ➤ **27**
    Voyageur Route: Sea-Kayaking for Canoeists 1.4 ➤ **33**
    The Outer Foxes 1.5 ➤ **41**
    The Bustards 1.6 ➤ **47**
**Section 2**
    The Eastern Shore 2.0 ➤ **53**
    The Churchill Islands 2.1 ➤ **55**
    Foster Island 2.2 ➤ **59**
    Naiscoot River Delta 2.3 ➤ **67**
    Hangdog Loop 2.4 ➤ **75**
    Bayfield Inlet to Pointe au Baril 2.5 ➤ **81**
    Franklin Island 2.6 ➤ **87**
    The McCoy Islands 2.7 ➤ **95**
    The Minks 2.8 ➤ **101**
    Moon Island Loop 2.9 ➤ **109**
    Sans Souci Loop 2.10 ➤ **115**
**Section 3**
    The Southern Bay 3.0 ➤ **125**
    Beausoleil Island 3.1 ➤ **127**
    Daytrips on the Southern Bay 3.2 ➤ **133**
**Section 4**
    The Bruce Peninsula 4.0 ➤ **135**
    Flowerpot Island 4.1 ➤ **139**
    Cabot Head to Tobermory 4.2 ➤ **147**
    Dyers Bay to Barrow Bay 4.3 ➤ **161**

References ➤ **168**

# ACKNOWLEDGMENTS

Writing this book would not have been possible without the assistance and help of many people. First we would like to thank Joan Barrett and Ted Moores of the Bear Mountain Boat Shop for their support and encouragement; Joan also came on a trip to the Minks with us and kindly found a rattlesnake for us to photograph. We would also like to thank Jonathon's cousin Paul Craig for paddling with us well into the cold fall weather. Thank you to Jonathon's parents for their support in all of our endeavors. Jonathon's mother even came on a research trip with us to Massasauga Provincial Park. Thank you to James Hunter and his daughter Meghan for paddling with us and our niece Sadie Brabant to Beausoleil Island.

A special thanks to all the people we met who helped us in our research: Tim Dyer at White Squall, Doug and Paula Cunningham, all the folks at Wildrock Outfitters for their help and generosity, Tim Watson for lending us maps on such short notice, and Aaron Lawton and Jennifer East at Killarney Outfitters. Thanks to Rachelle Laurin for doing our maps, and a special thanks to Terry Asma and Katrina Simmons for helping us out with our photos on very short notice. Thanks to Warren Edgar of Aloma Island for his hospitality. A big thank-you to Dan and Lucinda Travers, who stored our kayaks for us close to Georgian Bay so we didn't have to keep driving them back and forth.

Finally, we would like to thank Dagger, Cascade Designs, Werner Paddles, Lotus Designs, and Gaia for their support. It would have been hard to write this book without the support of all of these people. Thank you all.

# INTRODUCTION

Often called the Sixth Great Lake, Georgian Bay has a character uniquely its own. This large body of water, stretching 190 kilometers from north to south and 80 kilometers from east to west, is large enough to qualify as a Great Lake, but it was relegated to the status of a bay in 1819 by Lieutenant Henry Bayfield of the Royal Navy. Originally named Lake Manitoulin by Captain William Fitzwilliam Owen, it was later determined to be part of Lake Huron and was renamed after King George IV. No one thought to call it by the name the Wendat people gave it, Lake of Attigouatan. The Ojibwa on the northern shore called the bay Spirit Lake — which incidentally would translate to Lake Manitoulin, the name originally given it by Captain William Fitzwilliam Owen.

Georgian Bay is bounded on the north and east by the granite rocks and tangled bush of the Canadian Shield. The gouging and scouring action of the glaciers left behind thousands upon thousands of islands sprinkled thickly along the northern and eastern shores. The southern shore of Georgian Bay is much more pastoral, with sand beaches, farms and accompanying towns and cities. Westward, the shore of Georgian Bay is formed by the Bruce Peninsula, with the rugged limestone and dolomite of the Niagara Escarpment plunging into the deep, cold water. The deepest sounding on Georgian Bay is just off the shore near the tip of the Bruce Peninsula. The bottom slopes up from west to east with a few islands, such as the Limestone Islands and the Westerns, appearing far out on the bay waters. Manitoulin Island forms the northwestern boundary of Georgian Bay where the limestone crags of the Niagara Escarpment once again rise above the water.

One of North America's premier sea-kayaking destinations, Georgian Bay has a great deal to offer any paddler. Beauty, history, solitude, wilderness and an infinite variety of paddling conditions await the kayaker on the waters of Georgian Bay. *La Mer Douce,* "the sweetwater sea," as the French explorer Samuel de Champlain called Georgian Bay, was an important trade route for over two hundred years until it was supplanted by the railroad. Before Europeans ventured out onto the bay with their Native guides, those same Natives had lived on the shores of Georgian Bay for thousands of years. Some of their descendants still make their home along the shores of these beautiful waters.

The northern edge of Georgian Bay has been home to canoes for millennia, but canoes are not able to deal with the waves and weather that this freshwater sea is capable of brewing up. Sea kayaks allow us to explore more of this fascinating coastline in greater safety and comfort. Two advantages to paddling on the Great Lakes, as compared to paddling on the ocean, are the lack of tides and the abundance of fresh water for drinking.

It would be hard to design a landscape more suited to sea-kayaking than Georgian Bay. From the large waves and deep waters of the Bruce Peninsula, for the expert kayakers, to the sheltered waters in among the 30,000 Islands, for those just starting out in their kayaking careers, there is something for everyone on Georgian Bay. This landscape inspired the Group of Seven artists and is still inspiring people every day. The courier de bois and later the voyageurs called this land the *beau pays,* "the beautiful country," a name that still fits 200 years later. The proximity of such a large expanse of wilderness to major metropolitan centers such as Toronto and Buffalo add to the appeal of Georgian Bay as a sea-kayaking destination.

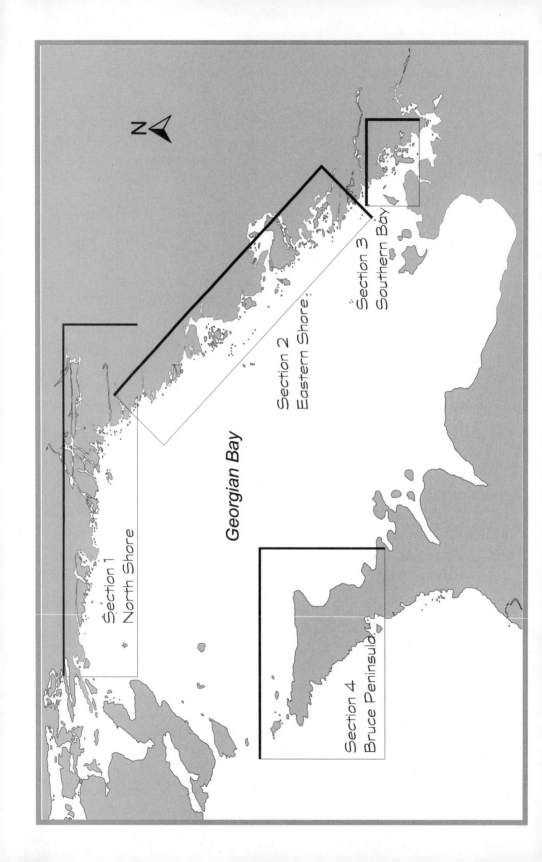

# THINGS TO KNOW ABOUT PADDLING ON GEORGIAN BAY

This book is not intended as an instruction manual for sea-kayak touring. We highly recommend that all novice kayakers attend a skills course before they paddle out on a trip. Make sure you have all the necessary safety equipment and know how to use it. Wear your life jacket — a good personal flotation device (PFD) is comfortable and can save your life. Listen to the long-range weather forecast before you leave on a trip and have alternate routes planned in case of extremely bad weather. Most of all, respect the land you are traveling through and have fun!

It is possible to paddle on Georgian Bay from May until late October, but the risk of hypothermia increases at either end of the paddling season. Hypothermia occurs when the body's core temperature is lowered, generally through exposure to cold water. The possibility of hypothermia exists throughout the paddling season everywhere on Georgian Bay. The greatest danger lies in the area off the Bruce Peninsula, due to the extremely deep water. Snow is a possibility in the spring and fall, and the worst storms are also generally in the spring and fall. Mosquitoes and blackflies can be quite ferocious on land in the early summer, but they are generally only really bad in the evening and early morning when the wind is low or still.

One of the hazards of sea-kayaking here is the slippery algae on most rocks at the water's edge. This algae can be very dangerous when you are getting in and out of the kayak and when loading the boats. In addition to the algae, the stone beaches, especially on the Bruce Peninsula, are quite difficult to walk on in bare feet or booties because the rocks tend to roll and slip, which can result in badly bruised ankles. Another shore hazard are the zebra mollusks, which have been invading the Great Lakes for the past ten to twenty years. Their extremely sharp shells can lacerate unprotected feet or hands. They are currently concentrated in the southern portion of Georgian Bay, but they are slowly invading northward. Zebra mollusks have no natural predators in these waters to keep their numbers in check, and without competition they are taking over the lake bottom.

Despite the apparent agelessness and rugged nature of this area, it is in fact a fragile environment. Those of us who plan on spending time enjoying the incredible beauty offered by this land must learn to take care of it and tread lightly upon it. For over one hundred years Georgian Bay has suffered the ravages of "progress." Gone are the huge white pines and the vast fish stocks. In their place we have cottages nestled in among second-growth forest — a recovering landscape and a fishery that has not recovered. It was the beauty of this area that ensured the eventual preservation of large areas. People who built summer cottages here did not want their summer sojourns ruined by a ruined environment, and since the turn of the century there have been cries for the preservation of Georgian Bay as a semi-wilderness preserve.

As sea-kayakers heading into this environment, we must do our part to ensure that we have as little impact on the land as possible. "No-trace camping" should be the rule whenever you camp in a non-developed area. Some areas, such as Beausoleil Island, sites in Bruce Peninsula National Park, Flowerpot Island and the campsites in Massasauga Provincial Park, are developed and have privy boxes, picnic tables and established fire rings. In these areas, use the facilities provided and please refrain from moving fire rings around.

On the rest of Georgian Bay, camping is still primitive wilderness camping. Many of the best spots — indeed in some areas the only spots — to pitch a tent are on flat granite. This means that a self-standing tent is necessary to camp easily in these areas. But the extremely strong westerly winds that often blow on Georgian Bay can cause problems. Camping on rock does not allow you to stake out your tent, but it is possible to safely anchor your tent using a few small stones or branches, short lengths of cord and larger rocks. First, take the cord and fasten half a meter to each tent-peg loop on your tent, then tie the small rocks or short branches to the end of this cord. By stretching the cord out and placing the larger rock on top of the cord, with the smaller stone keeping the cord from pulling out from under the rock, you can safely and securely keep your tent up and anchored against the wind.

Always keep your food out of your tent and, whenever possible, hang it out of reach of animals. Some kayakers keep their food in their kayaks at night, which is fine as long as your nocturnal visitors do not include bears. Remember, your kayak is your way off of whatever island you are camping on, and one angry swat from a bear can make the strongest kayak a submarine. Bears are not a common nuisance on Georgian Bay, but this is their home, so be prepared.

Another native inhabitant of this area is the Massasauga rattlesnake. Ontario's only venomous snake, these shy creatures will not bother you unless you threaten them or accidentally step on them. Count yourself lucky if you do get a chance to see one of these snakes, which are now listed as threatened on Canada's endangered species list. Poisonous plants are far more likely to cause you trouble on a trip on Georgian Bay, the most common being poison ivy. Learn how to identify this three-leaf plant. It can be just a couple of inches tall or as big as a bush, and it is always a bad experience.

Campfires are part of the whole mystique of camping, but they are also extremely detrimental to a fragile environment because they deplete precious dead wood that is needed to replenish soil nutrients for future plant growth. The extreme heat of a fire and quick cooling by dousing it with water can cause the granite to become brittle and friable and can leave damage that will be visible for millennia. If possible, use a stove for cooking and use the evening for stargazing instead of firegazing. In the summer months a fire is definitely not needed, and in the spring and fall you can limit yourself to a brief warming fire before turning in. It may seem as if there is lots of dead wood around, but imagine two hundred people using that same campsite over the course of one season and you will understand the impact that fires can have on an area. More and more people are using the wilderness and we must adapt our use to the increasing impact that we will have on the environment. If you really want a fire, consider bringing your own wood with you.

Finally, pack out everything that you pack in. Coming across garbage in the wilderness is a horrible experience. Since you will have no portages on a sea-kayaking trip, you do not have to carry your garbage any further than the kayak. You can find several excellent books on no-trace camping methods at most outdoor stores and libraries. Please take the time to learn from them so that future generations will also be able to enjoy paddling and camping on Georgian Bay. As the saying goes, "Take nothing but pictures and leave nothing but footprints."

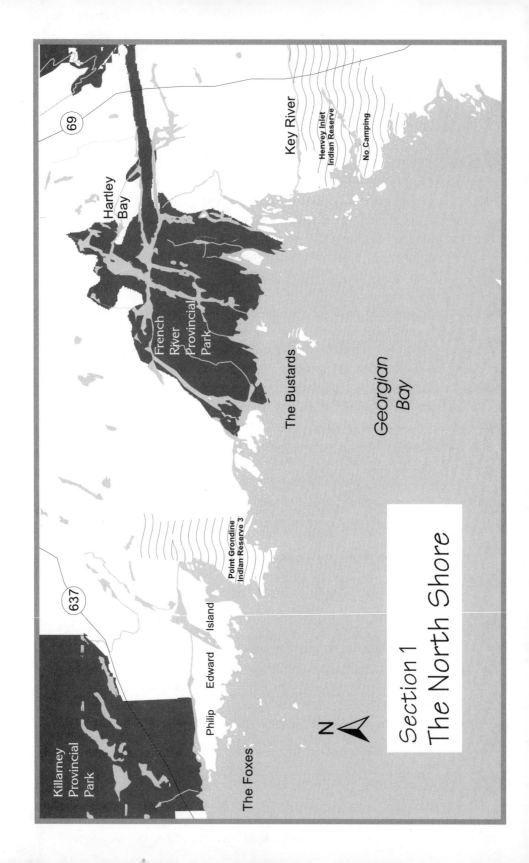

Killarney
Provincial
Park

637

69

Hartley
Bay

French
River
Provincial
Park

Key River

Henvey Inlet
Indian Reserve

No Camping

The Bustards

Georgian
Bay

Point Grondine
Indian Reserve 3

Philip Edward Island

The Foxes

N

Section 1
The North Shore

# THE NORTH SHORE 1.0

When you travel along the north shore of Georgian Bay, you are traveling in the footsteps of history. The route from the French River along the shoreline to Killarney has been used for hundreds of years as a major transportation link between east and west. Until the railway united Canada, this waterway was part of the most direct route west from the fledgling colonies. For centuries it was a trading and war route used by the Natives. The French were the first Europeans to use this route. From the early 1600s, when Champlain named Georgian Bay "La Mer Douce" (the sweetwater sea), an endless stream of explorers, courier de bois and voyageurs traveled these waters. The British and Americans fought over this coast as part of the War of 1812. But with the coming of the railroad and the decline in the timber industry, developers seemed to forget about this shoreline. That forgetfulness has preserved an exquisite and fragile environment for us to enjoy.

Because access to most of this shoreline is still limited to water access only, it remains relatively unpopulated. This combination of history, low population density and stunning landscape made up of the tortured granite of the Canadian Shield, gnarled white pines and cedars make this an excellent sea-kayaking destination.

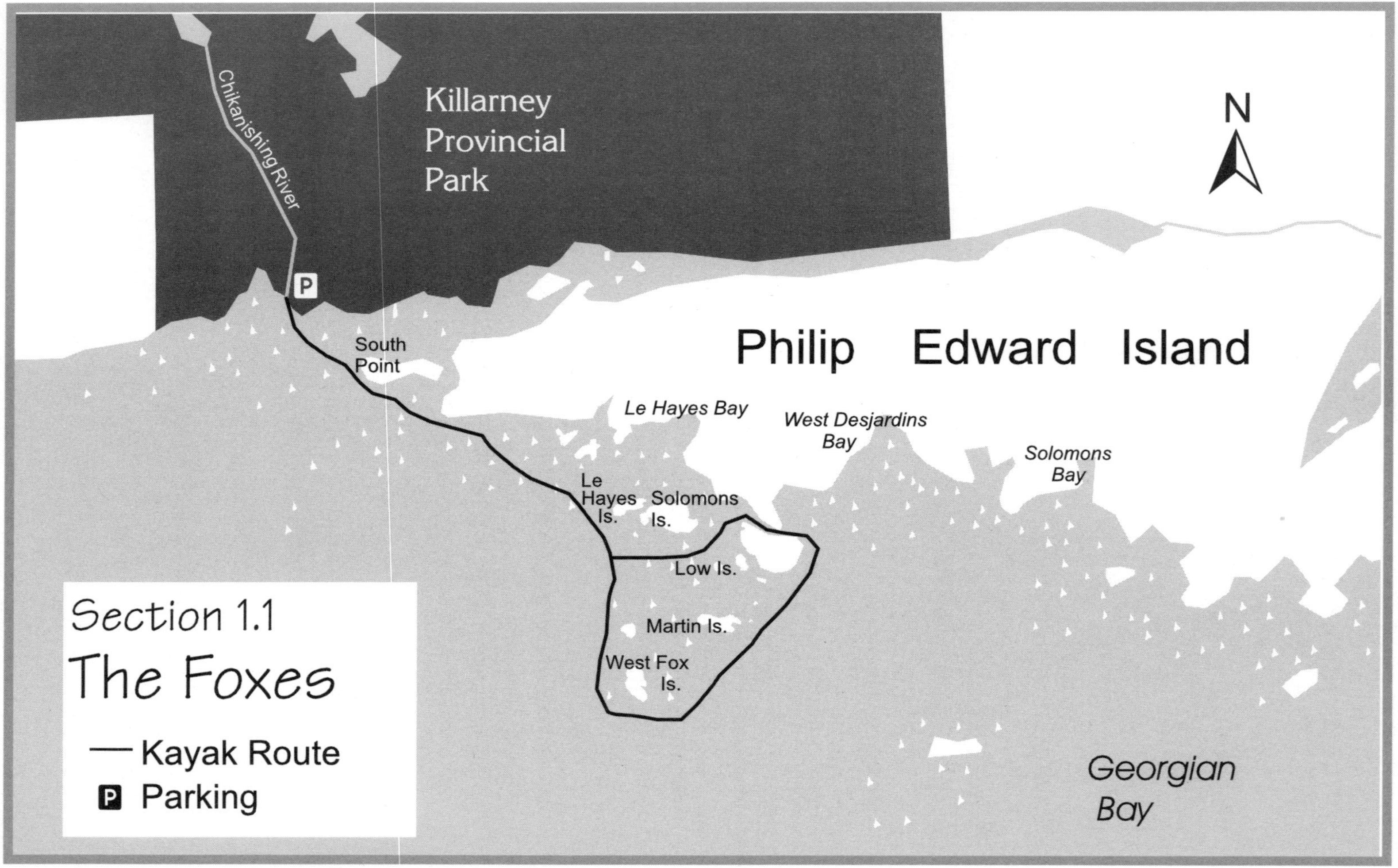

N

Killarney
Provincial
Park

Chikanishing River

South
Point

P

Philip   Edward   Island

Le Hayes Bay

West Desjardins
Bay

Solomons
Bay

Le
Hayes
Is.

Solomons
Is.

Low Is.

Martin Is.

West Fox
Is.

Georgian
Bay

Section 1.1
The Foxes
— Kayak Route
P Parking

# THE FOXES 1.1

Stretching south into Georgian Bay from the southwest shore of Phillip Edward Island is a small group of islands called the Foxes. The views of the La Cloche mountain range in Killarney Provincial Park are breathtaking from the Foxes. The Foxes make a wonderful three- to five-day trip from the access point of Chikanishing Creek in Killarney Provincial Park. These islands are made up of smoothly sculptured pink granite. On many of these islands, large kettles have been eroded into the sides of the rock, gently undulating in sensuous shapes. Whenever we paddle out to the Foxes, we are amazed at how the shapes of the water are mirrored in the granite. Curling, cresting granite waves have been waiting to break since the glaciers retreated. Smooth-flowing streams of rock, polished by the meltwaters of those same glaciers, have been frozen in time for 10,000 years. The Foxes as a whole are like a beautiful sculpture within which it is possible to paddle and explore. On West Fox Island there is a cobble-

*A beach on the Foxes.*

*Sculpted rock formations on the Foxes.*

stone beach that is a great picnic spot. Landing here can be quite treacherous in a west wind, however, since it is exposed to the full fury of Georgian Bay's prevailing westerlies.

We generally stay in the George Lake Campground at Killarney Provincial Park the first night so that we can get a full day's paddling in on our first day on the water. Killarney Outfitters rents kayaks by the day, so renters should leave in the morning to get a full day's use. If you decide to stay at the park the first night, make your reservation well in advance. Killarney is one of the most popular parks in Ontario and is extremely busy during the summer months.

Once on the water at Chikanishing Creek, paddle out onto the bay and head around the western end of Phillip Edward Island. To your right, a long shoal called the Long Rocks stretches to the southwest, and straight ahead are the Foxes. It is wise to hug the south shore of Phillip Edward Island and thread your way through the small islands, which offer shelter from the wind and waves. Once at the Foxes, we like to set up a base camp to use for the next few days.

There are many great exploratory paddles to be made around the Foxes, and it is worth getting out of your kayaks to spend some time exploring the rocky islands themselves. The Foxes are a popular destination for kayakers and as such are in danger of being too heavily used. Please take care to leave no trace of your visit to these beautiful islands. There are a few cottages on Low Island, so please respect the cottagers' privacy. Each of the islands in the Foxes has its own character, largely determined by the rock formations. For instance, the island due north of West Fox Island has incredible kettles that were carved in the rocks by glacial water swirling stones around and around in the same spot for ages. Often the stone that has done the most carving is still in the bottom of the kettle it carved. On the northeast corner of this island, the rock seems to flow in undulating waves down to the water's edge and under the surface to the boulder- and cobblestone-strewn bottom.

Spend at least a day, preferably two, exploring the coastlines of these islands by kayak. Carry your lunch with you and, in those ruggedly beautiful spots where it is not possible to camp, stop to eat, swim and explore, then return to your camp to watch the sun set over the white quartzite mountains of the La Cloche range. These mountains form the backdrop to all paddling on the Foxes. They are beautiful in the morning, tinged with the gold and pink of a new day, and provide a spectacular horizon over which the sun sets.

When you leave to return to Chikanishing Creek, take care to watch the weather. If you encounter a stiff west wind, it can be quite a challenging paddle back into the mouth of Collins Inlet and then into the mouth of the creek. It is often possible to use the numerous small islands and shoals that dot the southern edge of Phillip Edward Island as wind and wave breaks. The white mountains draw you on toward the creek mouth. Once you enter Chikanishing Creek you are surrounded by vegetation, and the mountains are no longer visible. Take your time paddling this stretch of water and look for wildlife. We have seen herons, frogs and water snakes on this short stretch of creek. Once back at the parking area, load up, pray that your battery isn't dead (ours has been), and head back home, taking a bit of the Foxes away with you in your memory.

## ACCESS:
Chikanishing Creek, Killarney Provincial Park. Take Highway 69 to Highway 637. Follow it to Killarney Provincial Park main office.

## ALTERNATE ACCESS:
It is also possible to leave from the town of Killarney, but the paddle out to the Foxes can be very exposed and treacherous.

## KAYAK AND GEAR RENTALS:
Killarney Outfitters, Killarney, Ontario, P0M 2A0
1-800-461-1117, 705-287-2828, fax 705-287-2691
E-mail KillarnMtn@aol.com
www.georgianbay.com/2003-001.htm

## MAPS:
1:50,000, Topographic Maps, Collins Inlet 41 H/14

## CHARTS:
Small Craft Charts, 2204

## FEES:
No camping fees, but parking fees payable to Killarney Provincial Park at Chikanishing Creek. $7.50/day or $50 for yearly pass. If you plan to spend your first or last night at George Lake Campground, it costs $19.75 in high season and $17.75 off-season. For information contact:
Killarney Provincial Park
Killarney, Ontario
P0M 2A0
705-287-2900 (information)
705-287-2800 (reservations) for George Lake Campground

## SPECIAL CONSIDERATIONS:
The Foxes are exposed to the full fury of westerly storms. Take the time to get a good weather forecast before heading out.

## DIFFICULTY:
Novice to intermediate paddling skills are required. The only real difficulty is high winds, which can maroon you on the islands for a day or two.

## TRIP LENGTH:
3 to 5 days, depending on how much exploring you do.

## POSSIBLE EXTENSIONS:
It is possible to extend this trip by paddling out to the Hawk Islands or exploring the south coast of Phillip Edward Island.

# PHILLIP EDWARD ISLAND 1.2

Phillip Edward Island is a large island on the coast of Georgian Bay just east of Killarney. A wonderful five- to seven-day loop trip is possible around the island. The inner passage, Collins Inlet, was once the water highway for the lumber town of Collins Inlet. This town was founded in 1886 and lasted until 1918, when the mill burned down and the ruins were salvaged for scrap metal for the First World War. All that is left are a few buildings that are now part of Mahzenazing Lodge.

Where once the schooners and tugs of the lumber trade sailed, a procession of pleasure boats now follow the well-marked channel up Collins Inlet to Beaverstone Bay and then out onto the open waters of Georgian Bay. Despite the number of boats using this channel, it is still a worthwhile paddle because it allows us to see a piece of the lumbering history of Georgian Bay and it is a very sheltered alternative to the outer side of Phillip Edward Island. The first 9 kilometers of the north shore of the inlet is part of Killarney Provincial Park and all park rules apply in this stretch.

*Philip Edward Island with the La Cloche mountains in the distance.*

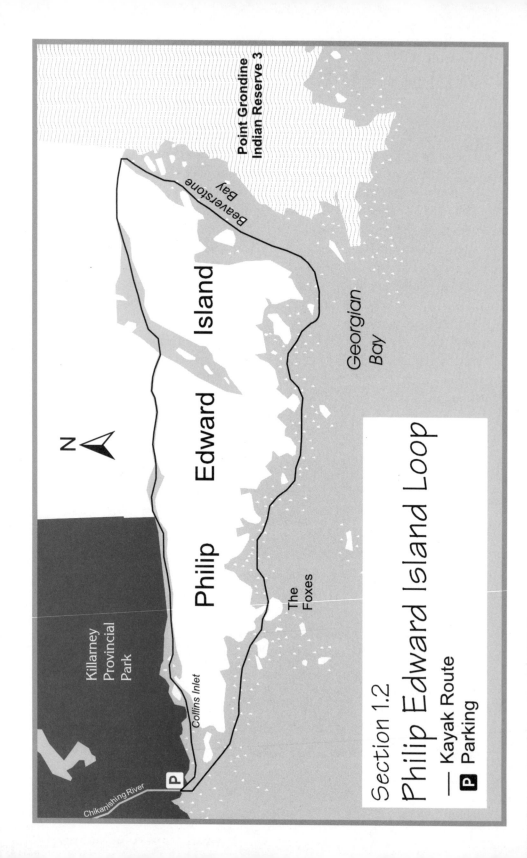

Section 1.2
Philip Edward Island Loop

— Kayak Route
P Parking

Killarney Provincial Park

Chikanishing River

Collins Inlet

Philip

Edward

Island

N

The Foxes

Georgian Bay

Beaverstone Bay

Point Grondine Indian Reserve 3

Phillip Edward Island itself and the rest of the shoreline is Crown land, with a few private cottages and lodges sprinkled along the shore. Please respect these cottagers' privacy and do not trespass on their land. There are many excellent camping spots all around Phillip Edward Island, far more of them on the outer shore than along the sheltered inside passage. One other restriction to camping in this area is the Point Grondine Indian Reserve. The entire eastern shore of Beaverstone Bay is part of this reserve and is off limits to camping. Despite these restrictions, camping should not be a problem anywhere on this route.

The access point for this trip is in Killarney Provincial Park, sometimes called the "Crown Jewel of Ontario Parks." This incredibly beautiful and popular park has an access point to Georgian Bay from Chikanishing Creek. We suggest camping in the campground at Killarney Provincial Park after the long drive into Killarney. It is a long way to Killarney from almost anywhere, which is one of the reasons why this area is still so beautiful and relatively pristine. If you are renting kayaks in Killarney, Killarney Outfitters rents their boats by the day so you are better off picking up the boats early in the morning. If you stay in the park's campground the first night, be sure to reserve a site well in advance. It is not uncommon for Killarney to be completely booked months ahead of time.

No matter what time you put your kayak in the water at Chikanishing Creek, you must make sure that you have paid for parking at this access point. If you plan to visit many provincial parks, we would advise investing in a parks pass, which will allow you to visit any provincial park in Ontario, as well as allow you to leave your car at the Chikanishing Creek access point. The pass is $50, or alternatively you can pay $7.50 per day to park your car at the access point. Once you have loaded up your kayak with everything you need for a week, park the car (in the shade if possible) and push off down the winding creek toward the open water of the bay.

As you hit the open water of the bay, the weather will determine your destination. Try to get a long-range forecast before you leave, so you have some idea of what to expect. If it is very windy, paddle the channel of Collins Inlet first, but if it is calmer and likely to get stormy later in the week, paddle the outside of the island first. It doesn't matter which way you go around Phillip Edward Island, both directions offer beautiful scenery.

*Rock formations on the west side of the French River delta.*

We generally try to paddle the inside of the island first so that if we have extra time we can spend it exploring the hundreds of little islands scattered along the outer edge of the island. Once out on the larger water of the inlet, turn east and paddle up the inlet past the few fishing camps and cottages. The channel is quite narrow here, so try to stay out of the main channel and away from any powerboats. On long weekends in particular there can be large numbers of powerboats motoring through this inlet. The channel cuts almost due east for 15 kilometers, where it opens out into Mill Lake.

Eighty years ago this was a very lively place, with log booms jamming the water and schooners (later steam vessels) bringing in supplies and mail. The old town site is on the northern edge of the lake, just east of Chicken Island. The town site is private now, so if you want to explore you must get permission from Mahzenazing Lodge. The main lodge building is the former boarding house for the town. There are many campsites along the edges of Mill Lake, and this is where we spend our first night. Sometimes Mill Lake can look like a small marina because it provides safe, sheltered anchorage for pleasure boats.

The following day, paddle further up the inlet and turn south into Beaverstone Bay. Remember that the eastern shore of Beaverstone Bay is part of Point Grondine Indian Reserve and is off limits for camping. Find a nice spot to camp on the western shore and enjoy your last night sheltered from the prevailing westerly winds. The rest of this route is exposed to the west wind, though it is always possible to find a sheltered spot on the lee side of the many islands that dot the southern shore of Phillip Edward Island.

Paddling out of Beaverstone Bay we disturbed hundreds of cormorants. It is thrilling to see and hear hundreds of these birds flying overhead and watch them running in ungainly fashion along the water in order to get up enough speed to take off. The cormorants are fairly new to Georgian Bay and are a close relative of the loon. We hope they will be able to coexist with the loon and not push the loons out of their habitat. The cormorants make Georgian Bay seem like part of the ocean, since they are primarily seabirds. At the mouth of Beaverstone Bay, turn west and paddle through the many rocks and shoals on the southern edge of the island. We generally camp somewhere around the Big Rock Portage. This portage has been here for centuries. It was originally a Native route, and then the fur traders used it to avoid paddling out in the bigger waves past Bateman Island.

The following day is spent exploring the coast between Bateman Island and the Foxes, a chain of islands stretching south into Georgian Bay. Of particular interest is West Desjardin Bay. This is a wonderful place to see fishers and the occasional otter. Be quiet, take your time, look closely, and you will be well rewarded with wildlife sightings in this area, particularly at dusk. The ability of the sea kayak to get into very shallow water makes it ideal for wildlife viewing.

Once ensconced on a comfortable campsite near the Foxes, plan to spend at least two days exploring the Foxes and, if the weather permits, the more distant Hawk Islands. The Foxes make an excellent weekend trip on their own (see The Foxes, Section 1.1), but they are also well worth spending the extra time to explore. If you do decide to visit the Hawk Islands on this trip, be aware of their exposure to the winds of the bay. It is very easy to get windbound on these islands, so even if you are just going for a daytrip, take enough supplies to carry you through till the next day, just in case. Also be aware that if you are leaving from the shelter of the Foxes for the Hawks, you will not appreciate the full force of the wind until you leave the wind shadow of the Foxes.

Waves can easily double in height as you leave the wind shadow of the Foxes. Green Island is well worth a visit if you are out on the Hawk Islands, because it has a completely different topography than the northern islands and is heavily wooded. It has no sheltered bays, however, so should be reserved for a calm day. From the south shore of Green Island, it is possible to see Papoose Island on the horizon, and after Papoose Island there is no land until the southern edge of Georgian Bay. It is a humbling experience to look south and see no land.

The last day of paddling takes us back into Chikanishing Creek. The stretch of water between the Foxes and the Long Rocks, at the western end of Phillip Edward Island, can be quite rough, but it is possible to island hop and hide behind the rocks and reefs most of the way back. As you paddle in, you will see the majestic white quartzite mountains of the La Cloche range rising behind the pink granite shoreline. It is a beautiful sight, especially on a calm, misty morning with the call of a loon echoing across the water.

*A windswept white pine is silhouetted against a flame-colored sky.*

## ACCESS:

Chikanishing Creek, Killarney Provincial Park. Take Highway 69 to Highway 637. Follow it to Killarney Provincial Park main office.

## ALTERNATE ACCESS:

It is also possible to leave from the town of Killarney, but the paddle out to Phillip Edward Island can be very exposed and treacherous.

## KAYAK AND GEAR RENTALS:

Killarney Outfitters, Killarney, Ontario, P0M 2A0
1-800-461-1117, 705-287-2828, fax 705-287-2691
E-mail KillarnMtn@aol.com
www.georgianbay.com/2003-001.htm

## MAPS:

1:50,000, Topographic Maps, Collins Inlet 41 H/14

## CHARTS:

Small Craft Chart, 2204

## FEES:

No camping fees, but parking fees at Chikanishing Creek. $7.50/day or $50 for yearly pass.

## SPECIAL CONSIDERATIONS:

There can be considerable boat traffic on Collins Inlet, especially during long weekends. Respect the Native reserve and the private cottages.

## DIFFICULTY:

Novice to intermediate paddling skills are required. The only real difficulty would be high winds on the south shore of the island.

## TRIP LENGTH:

7 to 10 days, depending on how much exploring you do. It can be done in 5 days, but that leaves no room for windbound days.

## POSSIBLE EXTENSIONS:

It is possible to extend this trip by paddling further east to the mouth of the French River and the Bustard Islands. Count on another week of paddling at least to do this.

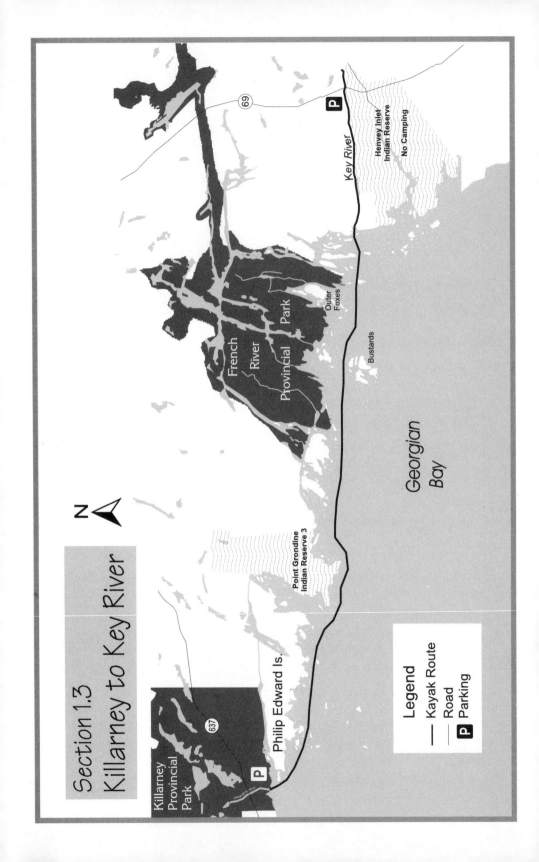

# KILLARNEY TO KEY RIVER 1.3

A long the stretch of coastline from Killarney to Key River you will be paddling what was the main route from east to west before the completion of the railway. Every spring a flotilla of canoes would travel this route on their way from Montreal to Grand Portage, and later to Fort William on Lake Superior. The influence of these French-Canadian voyageurs is still evident in the place names along this shore: Point Grondine, La Cloche, West Desjardin Bay and, of course, the French River. Long before the Europeans came to claim these lands for a distant and often uninterested king, the local Natives used these waterways to pursue trade and war. Some of their descendants still live in the area at the Point Grondine Indian Reserve. This shoreline has changed little in the time since Etienne Brûlé first set eyes on these waters in the early 1600s. He loved the area so much that he never returned to New France, choosing instead to spend the rest of his life using this region as his base.

It is generally best to paddle this route from west to east due to the prevailing winds, which are westerlies here. Killarney Outfitters offers a shuttle service for a fee from Killarney to Key River and vice versa. Contact them well in advance to arrange this service. Once your return

*Key Harbour Lighthouse on the North Shore.*

shuttle has been arranged or you have dropped off your car at the Key Marine Resort in Key River, you are ready to head out onto the bay. It is possible to leave directly from Killarney, but the preferred departure point is from the Chikanishing Creek put-in at Killarney Provincial Park. Paddle down the creek, keeping an eye peeled for herons and water snakes, then glide out into the western entrance of Collins Inlet. If the weather is really nasty, it is possible to take Collins Inlet around Phillip Edward Island and stay in sheltered water for the first day's paddle.

If you are blessed with good weather, continue straight across the boat channel, keeping a good lookout for motorboats, and paddle around South Point on the tip of Phillip Edward Island. Depending on what time you get out on the water, you may want to head straight for the Foxes to find a spot to camp. The Foxes are a chain of islands that extend south into Georgian Bay from the south side of Phillip Edward Island. The granite on these islands has been shaped by glacial scouring into sinuous, sensual shapes that remind us of Henry Moore sculptures. If you look closely at the rock, it seems to portray in granite the flow of water and the rise and fall of swelling waves.

From the Foxes you have two options on your eastward course. If you are experienced and the weather is favorable, the Hawk Islands are a 2-kilometer crossing southeast from the Foxes. The shortest crossing from the Hawk Islands back to shore is another 2 kilometers, so be prepared for a long, hard paddle if the wind is not favorable. The other option is to follow the Foxes back to the shore of Phillip Edward Island and paddle through the many shoals and tiny islets toward the point of land crossed by Big Rock Portage. To the east of this point are Bateman Island and Hamilton Island, both of which are private and have several cottages on them. Four kilometers past Bateman Island, you come to the mouth of Beaverstone Bay, which marks the end of Phillip Edward Island. Across the bay, on the mainland, is the Point Grondine Indian Reserve. This is private land and off limits to campers, so time your night stops to be either here, on the western side of Beaverstone Bay, or 10 kilometers further along, past the Indian reserve.

The shoreline of Point Grondine Reserve is fringed with a delightful archipelago of tiny islands called the Chickens, which are divided by small channels for a couple of kilometers. Those of you paddling fiberglass kayaks and leery of getting scratches on them will have to exercise caution when exploring these channels. There are one or two spots where it is possible to camp in this group of islets if this is where the end of the day catches you. As long as you stay off the mainland, you are not trespassing on the Point Grondine Reserve. The islands in this area are all Crown land.

Once you round Point Grondine, for which the reserve is named, you will see across a large bay the westernmost exit of the French River, the Voyageur Channel. This bay can be quite treacherous when it is windy, due to the shallow shelves of rock throughout the bay, which cause waves to become very steep, choppy and confused. On calm days paddling across this bay and looking down at the bottom makes you feel as if you are flying over plateaus and canyons formed of flowing granite. The Voyageur Channel is named for the voyageurs who used this route on their way west to Grand Portage and east back to Montreal. This was the end of their struggles with wind and waves on the Great Lakes system, Lake Nipissing being the only large body of water to cross between here and Montreal. The Voyageur Channel is a sea-kayaking playground of sheltered pools, shallow and deep channels, long islands rising out of the water like the backs of migrating stone monsters. We have watched mink come right into our campsite here, and otters, gulls, terns, loons and cormorants are common. You will see very little motorized boat traffic because of the dangerous shoals. A few fishermen frequent the area, but for the most part you will have this wonderland all to yourself.

Green Island forms the eastern shore of the Voyageur Channel and must be skirted on one side or the other. The northern channel around the island is sheltered and quite marshy, so it is a great birdwatching spot. The southern side is defined by White Rock Ledge and White Rock. These get their name from guano deposits made by the cormorants, loons, terns and gulls, so don't think of stopping for a lunch break on one of them. If the weather is anything but extremely nasty, we would recommend the southern side, then continuing along the coast of Georgian Bay toward Bottle Island and the long fiord-like channels. On a sunny day, many of the small islands near Bottle Island sparkle from the quartz crystals embedded in the granite. Geologists will love this section of the paddle.

Past Bottle Island you enter Lodge Channel, which leads into the Bad River Channel, one of the western outlets of the French River. This area is quite popular with both the powerboat and cruising sailboat crowd, so be careful when paddling in the boating channels. The big attraction here is safe anchorage in a wild and rugged setting. The rapids on the Bad River range from tame to quite dangerous, depending on water levels and time of year.

The Gauthier Fisheries operated here from 1896 until 1969. All that is left of the large fish-processing plant are a few pilings and some rusting metal on the shore. The Gauthiers own Canada Dry Bottling Ltd. out of Windsor, Ontario, and used to fly back and forth in one of the first float planes in the area. There are still a few fishing camps in the area, and their boats cruise to the hot fishing spots in the mornings and return in the evenings, the sound of the motors echoing the buzz of the mosquitoes that come out at dusk.

The mouth of the Bad River Outlet is about halfway between Killarney and Key River. The Northeast Passage divides the mainland shore from the Bustard Islands, a few kilometers offshore — well worth spending a day exploring. If you don't go to the Bustards, your course lies across the mouth of the main outlet of the French River. At one time there was a large lumbering town here, but all that remains is a small fishing camp, the lighthouse, boilers and a few stone foundations overgrown with trees. Georgian Bay has taken back the land and covered the scars that man left behind from construction during the lumber boom. There is also a small, very hard-to-find cemetery that has a few weathered gravestones. Across the channel there are a few iron rings in the rocks and some pilings still sprouting from the water. As you paddle east through the islands on the north shore of the Northeast Passage, you may well see otters playing and fishing.

The Bustard Islands will give way on your right to open water stretching south, broken only by the white-daubed Gull Rocks. On the north shore are the Outer Fox Islands, which are well worth camping at and exploring. This stretch of paddling can also be done in the shelter of small channels threaded through the islands scattered along the shore of the French River Delta. Dead Island is in the distance as you paddle away from the Outer Fox Islands and is your next destination. Dead Island is Crown land now, but ownership is currently being disputed by the local Native band because there is a Native burial ground on it. Please respect the memory of the Natives buried there and camp on either the land on the north side of Dead Island Channel or on Dokis Island. The boat traffic through Dead Island Channel can be quite heavy on weekends, especially in the morning and late afternoon.

The last day of paddling takes you off Georgian Bay and up the Key River. Key Harbour, at the mouth of the Key River, was once a large shipping port, but the loading docks burned down and were never rebuilt. It is now a small cottage community. There is a public phone outside the small store and marina here, but that is the limit of services available. There is no road access and the rail lines were torn up long ago. Paddling up the river is a very different experience from paddling out on the open waters of the bay, but it has its own appeal. This trip can be filled with wildlife or with motorboats, depending on the time of day, week and year. Weekdays in spring, early summer and fall are the least busy times.

Once you can hear the highway, you are almost finished your trip. Paddling under Highway 69 marks your return to the world of cars and modern civilization.

ACCESS:
Chikanishing Creek, Killarney Provincial Park. Take Highway 69 to Highway 637. Follow it to Killarney Provincial Park main office. Key River is right on Highway 69.

ALTERNATE ACCESS:
It is also possible to leave from the town of Killarney, but that trip can be very exposed and treacherous.

KAYAK AND GEAR RENTALS:
Killarney Outfitters, Killarney, Ontario, P0M 2A0
1-800-461-1117, 705-287-2828, fax 705-287-2691
E-mail KillarnMtn@aol.com
www.georgianbay.com/2003-001.htm
Killarney Outfitters will also arrange a shuttle service for you. Contact them for details.

MAPS:
1:50,000, Topographic Maps, Collins Inlet 41 H/14 & Key River

CHARTS:
Small Craft Chart, 2204

FEES:
No camping fees but parking fees payable to Killarney Provincial Park at Chikanishing Creek. $7.50/day or $50 for yearly pass. If you plan to

*A sailing kayak near Deadman's Channel.*

spend your first or last night at George Lake Campground, it costs $19.75 in high season and $17.75 off-season. For information contact:
Killarney Provincial Park
Killarney, Ontario
P0M 2A0
705-287-2900 (information)
705-287-2800 (reservations) for George Lake Campground

**SPECIAL CONSIDERATIONS:**
Count on at least two days of windbound weather. Help can be a long way away.

**DIFFICULTY:**
Novice to intermediate paddling skills are required. The only real difficulty would be high winds that can maroon you for a day or two.

**TRIP LENGTH:**
7 to 9 days, depending on how much exploring you do.

**POSSIBLE EXTENSIONS:**
It is possible to extend this trip by exploring the Churchill Islands to the south of Key River.

# VOYAGEUR ROUTE: SEA-KAYAKING FOR CANOEISTS 1.4

This is the only route we have included that involves carrying kayaks over a portage. There are two portages, both quite short, and one is avoidable if water levels are in your favor. Too much water can be as bad as too little because high water levels can make these rapids extremely dangerous. We find this trip is a great one for people who have experience paddling a canoe and are comfortable on lakes and rivers but aren't too sure about the bigger, wide-open water often involved in sea-kayaking. This trip starts in the sheltered bays and channels of the Lower French River and then graduates to the open water at Batt Bay on Georgian Bay.

From the landing at Hartley Bay House, paddle west toward Wanapitei Bay. This area is home to many old lodges and camps. The oldest is the Kentucky Club, founded in 1912 as a gentleman's club by several sportsmen from Kentucky; it still runs as it was originally estab-

*Windswept pines on the delta of the French River.*

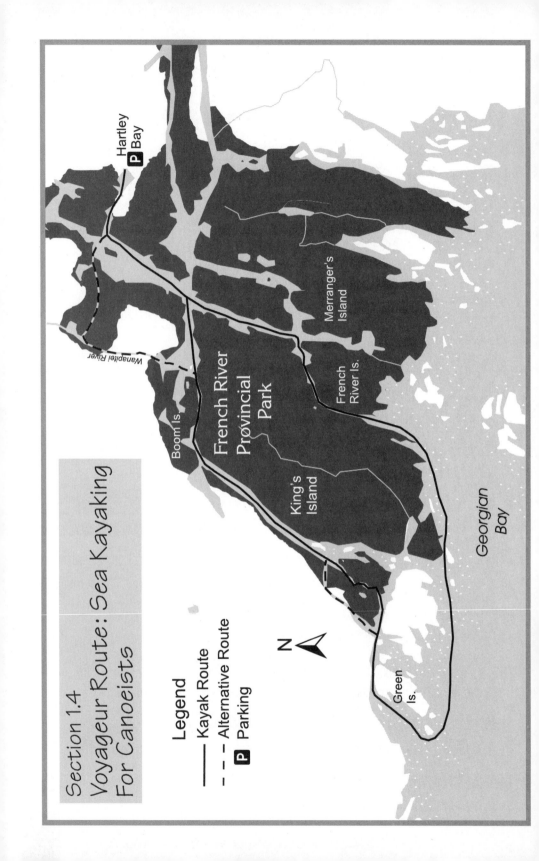

Section 1.4
Voyageur Route: Sea Kayaking
For Canoeists

Legend
— Kayak Route
– – Alternative Route
P Parking

N

Hartley
P Bay

Wanapitei River

Boom Is.

French River
Provincial Park

King's Island

Merranger's
Island

French
River Is.

Georgian
Bay

Green
Is.

lished. Because of the cottages and lodges in this area of the French River, there is a lot of motorboat traffic (especially early-morning fishermen) so be careful, especially in Hartley Bay and Wanapitei Bay.

Depending on water levels, it is also possible to paddle up the east fork of the Wanapitei River and down the west fork into Thompson Bay. This is a particularly good route to take if there is a strong headwind on Wanapitei Bay. To get to this alternate route, paddle north of Kentucky Club Island and continue along a gently turning river to the forks and let the current take you down to Thompson Bay.

Once on the Western Channel of the French River, paddle west through McCullums Narrows. Find a campsite in this area and prepare yourself for the next day. You are now on the historic route of the voyageurs. These men paddled 36-foot-long "canots de maître" loaded with trade goods and fur through these same waters from the early 1700s to the mid-1800s. Often there were flotillas of up to 50 of these large canoes on their way from Montreal to Grand Portage on the western end of Lake Superior. The route that they followed had the fewest portages and was the most sheltered from the winds of Georgian Bay. We follow the same route for somewhat different reasons. There is far less boat traffic on this route because of the shallow water near Georgian Bay and the hundreds of islands along the coast: what makes motorboat navigation difficult makes this area a delight to kayak through.

The second day, the route follows the French River Western Channel to a point where the river splits up into a number of channels. Read your map carefully in this area. It is very easy to get mixed up in the many different channels here. Some of these channels lead to major rapids and a few lead to watery cul-de-sacs. These cul-de-sacs are a lot of fun to explore and are great places to watch herons stalking their dinner, but they won't get you any closer to the open waters of Georgian Bay.

There are two channels to chose from here to get to Batt Bay or Green Island Bay: the furthest west (the Voyageur Route) leads into Black Bay and at low-water times may require two short portages; the other channel is the Old Voyageur Route. This is my favorite, as no motorboats can navigate this route, so it is quiet and quite wild. After a couple of kilometers of threading through small islands and following the current into tiny bays on the Old Voyageur Route, you'll reach the first portage. It is not always necessary to portage the 20 meters or so around a sharp drop over a ledge, depending on the height of the water. We have run this lit-

*Campsite near the outlet of the Voyageur Channel.*

tle drop, but there is a sharp left turn needed at the bottom. If you miss the turn, that could mean major damage to the kayak and maybe yourself. Remember, sea kayaks are not as maneuverable as whitewater kayaks: *Be careful!* Help could be a long way away.

After this portage there is a delightful coast down a kilometer-long chute ending at Balls Point. A word of caution, though: with low water levels there is a tricky right turn right at the end of this chute. It is not dangerous, but you may bump a rock or two if you miss the right channel. After this point, head west along a cross channel and paddle into an area of marsh. Among the pickerel weeds and water lilies, herons and Eastern kingbirds abound. A couple of kilometers from Balls Point comes your first view of the open water of Georgian Bay. Batt Bay and Green Island Bay are filled with literally hundreds of sculpted rock islands. Find a site and settle in to watch a beautiful sunset. These rocks were sculpted into fantastic curved shapes by glaciers thousands of years before. We spent one whole day just paddling around and exploring this area, watching the gulls and terns swoop and dive — and staying out in the wind in order to avoid the mosquitoes.

Wood is scarce on the outer islands, so if possible don't have a fire. If you do need a fire, have a small one and erase the evidence when you leave. This area is becoming more popular every year, and with more people using the area, the slim resources are being stretched to their limits. From this point, on a clear day you can see the La Cloche mountains around Killarney to the west. These quartzite mountains were once higher than the Rocky Mountains before the glaciers ground them down to their present height. They are stunningly beautiful, especially with the tops glowing in the last of the day's light. Once the sun has set, the stars wink into existence until they cover the sky in a blanket of jewels.

From Batt or Green Island Bay, head east toward the mouth of the main outlet of the French River. If the wind is right, this is a great stretch to paddle, surfing along the waves with the wind at your back and the sun beating down. The waves can get large very rapidly and you must watch for barely submerged rocks, which can be dangerous if you are in the trough of a wave as you paddle over them. We recommend this route be traveled in the counterclockwise direction because of the prevailing westerly winds, which are common here. What can be a great day coasting with the winds in one direction would be a hard day paddling in the other direction. For those new to sea-kayaking, this day of paddling is generally the day that they get hooked on kayak touring. Waves that would be scary to paddle through in a canoe are a lot of fun to play in while kayaking. It's in this kind of water that a sea kayak comes into its own. If the wind and waves are too rough and you are tight for time, it is possible to thread your way through the hundreds of islands scattered along the coast without leaving yourself overly exposed to the full impact of the wind and waves. If you have extra time, this is a good spot to paddle over to the Bustard Islands (see trip description on the Bustards, Section 1.6, for details).

As you get closer to the French River Main Channel, start looking for a campsite. One of my favorite sites is also a likely spot to see river otters. Heather and I sat, entranced, watching for almost an hour as two otters played and fed just off the shore from our campsite. They were very curious and kept coming closer and closer, diving, popping their heads up, snuffling and grunting and diving again. They eventually disappeared, but the magic they left behind stayed with us through the night.

The final day of this trip involves the only true portage. Think about this carry when you pack up the kayak in the morning. If at least a third of the weight in the kayak can be easily removed and carried 180 meters, then the portage around Dalles Rapids will be much easier. From your campsite, paddle north up the Main Channel of the French River past Camp McIntosh. This camp has been here since 1946, when it was built by Jim and Loretta McIntosh. They sold it in 1973 to the Thompsons, who have kept the original name. If you want a really relaxing night, it is possible to stay at Camp McIntosh rather than tenting for your last night.

On the eastern shore of the river is the old site of the original French River Village. In the 1880s the town boasted a population of 1,400 with an additional 500 seasonal workers. French River Village consisted of the mills of the Ontario Lumber Company, houses, boarding houses, a doctor's office, library, two churches (Roman Catholic and Presbyterian), two schools (public and separate), a jail and three hotels. Millions of board feet of lumber were milled here and the enormous piles of sawdust and scrap lumber were used to level the streets and fill in the rocky gullies in and near the town. All that is left of this town are a few brick walls from the jail, some rusting machinery from the lumber mills and the now automated lighthouse. There are also two small graveyards where it is possible to find a few headstones, one of which is for a baby girl who died in 1906. In 1922 the Company store closed for good and the era of logging ended on the French River shortly after that.

Dalles Rapids at the end of MacDougal Bay on the French River Main Channel is the site of the portage for which you carefully packed in the morning. These rapids have changed dramatically due to the actions of the Ontario Government. In the early 1960s the rapids were blown up in a huge explosion in an attempt to control the water level on the Upper French and Pickerel Rivers. The result was a decrease in the water level upstream from the rapids and a difficult whitewater run created from what had been a passable run. Since you are coming from Georgian Bay, it is necessary to portage no matter what the rapids are like. From the end of the portage, paddle to a junction of waterways called the Elbow (about 2 kilometers) and then turn north up the Main Channel of the French River. This will take you back to Wanapitei Bay and Hartley Bay, where your car awaits you.

## ACCESS:

Chikanishing Creek, Killarney Provincial Park. Take Highway 69 to Highway 637. Follow it to Killarney Provincial Park main office. Key River is right on Highway 69.

## ALTERNATE ACCESS:

It is also possible to leave from the town of Killarney but that trip can be very exposed and treacherous.

## KAYAK AND GEAR RENTALS:

Killarney Outfitters, Killarney Ontario, P0M 2A0
1-800-461-1117, 705-287-2828, fax 705-287-2691
E-mail KillarnMtn@aol.com
www.georgianbay.com/2003-001.htm
or White Squall, RR 1 Nobel, Ontario, P0G 1G0
705-324-5324 or 705-746-4936 fax 705-342-1975
www.zeuter.com/squall/

## MAPS:

Ministry of Natural Resources: *French River Provincial Park* is an excellent map available from many outfitters as well as directly from:
Sudbury District Office
Ministry of Natural Resources
3767 Highway 69 South, Suite 5
Sudbury, Ontario, P3G 1E7
705-522-7823
Canadian Topographic Maps 1:50,000:
41 I/2, 41 H/14, 41 H/15 1:50,000

## CHARTS:

Small Craft Chart, 2204

## FEES:

No camping fee, but it costs to leave your car at Hartley Bay Lodge.

## SPECIAL CONSIDERATIONS:

There are two portages on this route.

## DIFFICULTY:

Novice. This is an ideal first trip.

## TRIP LENGTH:

4 to 6 days, depending on how much exploring you do.

## POSSIBLE EXTENSIONS:

It is possible to extend this trip by exploring the Bustard Islands.

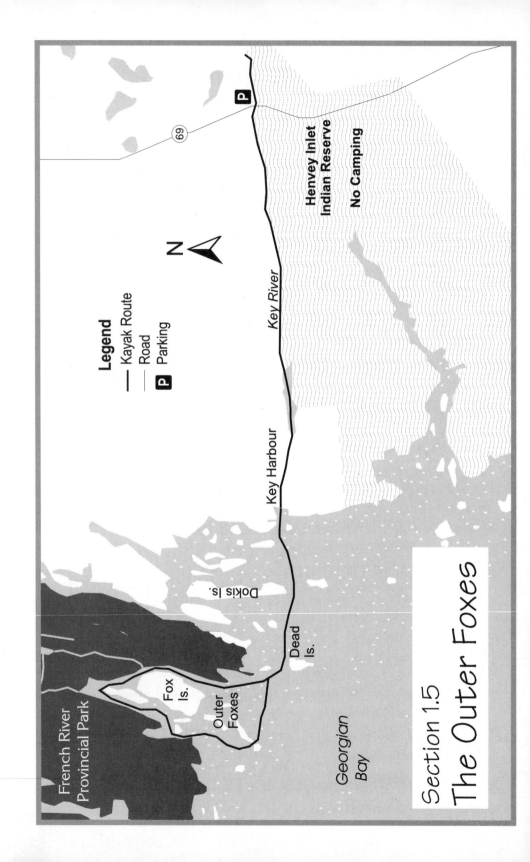

Section 1.5
The Outer Foxes

# THE OUTER FOXES 1.5

A sprinkling of granite rocks swathed in white breaking waves with a stunted tree-line acting as a backdrop is all that is visible of the Outer Fox Islands from the open water of Georgian Bay. Perhaps it is because of this less-than-welcoming appearance that the islands are still so unpopulated. You will probably see some fishermen, maybe one or two canoeists and fellow kayakers, but that is all the evidence of humanity you are likely to find in this rugged chain of islands extending north into the land between the French and Pickerel Rivers. The granite rocks that fringe the southern edge of these islands are called the Shirt Tails, and these boat-eating rocks ensure that few motorboats will venture into these treacherous waters. In the narrow channels and shallows of this island chain, the sea kayak excels at slipping into small bays, channels and inlets that most other craft cannot. The real magic of the Outer Fox Islands is found in these channels. Great blue herons, cormorants, loons, terns, gulls, mink and, of course, foxes are some of the Native inhabitants of these islands. The secluded waterways that stretch north into the

*Soaking up the silence on the Outer Foxes.*

mainland support moose and deer along with many different species of birds. This is a truly spell-binding area waiting to be explored.

The best access to the Outer Fox Islands is through Key River on Highway 69. There is a marina on Key River (Key Marine Resort) at which it is possible to park your vehicle for a small fee and paddle down the river out onto Georgian Bay. It is also possible to get a boat shuttle from Key River on Highway 69 to Key Harbour on Georgian Bay — a distance of 13 kilometers — but you must arrange this service well in advance through the folks at Key Marine Resort.

If you are not being shuttled out, it is a good idea to spend the night before your departure at Grundy Lake Provincial Park. The park is just a few kilometers north of Key River just off Highway 69. By spending the night at Grundy Lake Provincial Park, you have the advantage of getting in a full day's paddle on your first day on the water. There are a few places to camp on the north side of the Key River, but the south side is part of the Henvey Inlet Indian Reserve and is off-limits to camping. If you have the time, it is definitely better to stay at the park and then spend a complete day to paddle the 18 to 20 kilometers out to the first good camping on the south end of Dokis Island or on the mainland north of Dead Island. It is possible to paddle all the way to the Outer Fox Islands in one day, but finding a campsite late at night on these rugged islands could be a challenge.

Leaving Dokis Island in the morning you will pass through Dead Island Channel. Dead Island is the site of an ancient Native burial ground, so please respect their memory and show your respect from a distance. Once through Dead Island Channel it is possible to turn north and wend your way through long, narrow, almost sinuous granite islands. Make sure that you have truly left the Dead Island Channel before you make your turn. There is one particularly long inlet that dead-ends after more than 2 kilometers of paddling. If you do make this mistake, it is possible to carry your kayaks over the smooth, rounded rock to the true channel about 100 meters further west. We recommend that you find a campsite reasonably early and use it as a base for daytrips to explore the rest of the Outer Foxes.

One excellent daytrip from the Outer Fox Islands is a paddle around Fox Island to the northeast. This can also be a good chance to move camp if your initial site was not as good as you were hoping for. There are four prime campsites at the north end of Fox Island that are very shel-

*A cormorant in a tree.*

tered from the winds coming off Georgian Bay. Take the time to explore the many long, narrow inlets running deep into the land. These small inlets are the result of glacial action and are home to a host of bird life. One channel, the entrance of which is about a kilometer west of Vixen Island, can take you almost 6 kilometers into the interior. Most of these channels are too narrow or shallow at some point for even the smallest motorboat, so you will likely have them all to yourself. A quiet paddle through this area will almost always be rewarded with sightings of mink, herons and several types of ducks. We have been able to paddle within a few feet of the very shy great blue heron in this inlet.

After a day spent exploring north, in toward the mainland, a day spent exploring the coast to the west is a very different experience. There are more cottages and a couple of larger fishing lodges in this direction. One of these will be quite obvious, with the cottages all painted white with red trim. This is Georgian Bay Fishing Camp and is the largest fishing camp in this area. There is a good channel to the north of the camp that will take you past Dock Island and through Parting Channel into the wide mouth of the French River. The old town site is completely overgrown now, but there is still a lighthouse on the river. Looking south you will see the Bustard Islands.

After a lunch on a rocky island, it is time to turn your kayak back toward the Outer Fox Islands and your waiting campsite. If the weather is calm enough or if you like playing in the waves, the route through the many small islands fringing the edge of the bay makes an exhilarating paddle. With a west wind, your view of the Outer Fox Islands as they become visible through the myriad of other islands dotting the edge of the Northeast Passage will be of what looks like impassable rocky reefs foaming with white, crashing waves. There is a way through them, which will become clear as you paddle closer and the waves calm down once you are in the shelter of those rocks.

It is possible to paddle the entire distance from the Outer Fox Islands to the take-out point at Key River, but it makes for a very long day. If you have the time, break it into two days and camp on Dokis Island on your last night. You will retrace your steps up the Key River on the last day. As you paddle the last few kilometers up the Key River, the magic of the Outer Fox Islands fades away, but a little of it stays with all who spend a few days absorbing it.

ACCESS:
Marina put-in just north of the bridge on Highway 69 over the Key River. They charge a small fee for parking and can also arrange for boat shuttle service out onto Georgian Bay.
Contact Key Marine Resort, Gil Gariup, RR 1 Britt, Ontario, P0G 1A0
705-383-2422 fax 705-383-2282

KAYAK AND GEAR RENTALS:
White Squall, RR 1 Nobel, Ontario, P0G 1G0
705-324-5324 or 705-746-4936 fax 705-342-1975
www.zeuter.com/squall/

MAPS:
1:50,000, Topographic Maps, Key Harbour 41 H/15

CHARTS:
Small Craft Charts, 2204

FEES:
Small fee for parking at Key Marine Resort. Camping at Grundy Lake Provincial Park costs $19.75/night

RADIO STATION FOR MARINE REPORT:
88.9, but it is very weak at this range.

SPECIAL CONSIDERATIONS:
An excellent trip for wildlife viewing.

DIFFICULTY:
Novice to intermediate, depending on the weather conditions.

TRIP LENGTH:
4 to 7 days

POSSIBLE EXTENSIONS:
Explore the hundreds of islands along the many outlets of the French River and the Bustards: see Section 1.6.

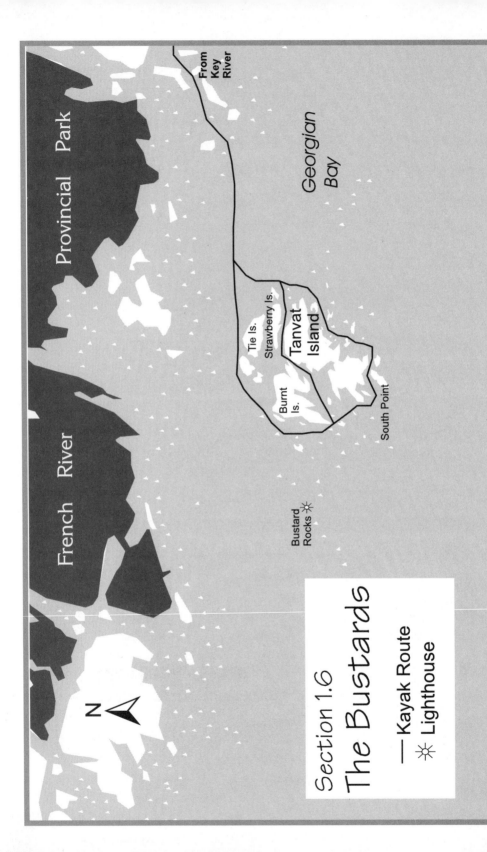

French River

Provincial Park

From
Key
River

Georgian
Bay

Tie Is.
Strawberry Is.

Tanvat
Island

Burnt
Is.

South Point

Bustard
Rocks ☀

N

Section 1.6
The Bustards

— Kayak Route
☀ Lighthouse

# THE BUSTARDS 1.6

The Bustard Islands, commonly called the Bustards, are a tightly clustered group of islands 2 to 3 kilometers south of the main outlet of the French River. These islands were among the busiest fishing stations on Georgian Bay until the 1950s, when the fish stocks plummeted and the fishery died. Many of the cottages on the Bustards are owned by the descendants of the early fishermen. Many of these fishermen came from the south shore of Georgian Bay, and some of the islands, like Meaford Island, are named after the towns that these men lived in during the winter.

The easiest access to the Bustards is through Key River on Highway 69. There is a marina on Key River (Key Marine Resort) where you can park your vehicle for a small fee and from there, paddle down the river out onto Georgian Bay. It is possible to arrange a boat shuttle from Key River on Highway 69 to Key Harbour on Georgian Bay — a distance of 13 kilometers — but you need to arrange this service well in advance through the folks at Key Marine Resort. If you are not being shuttled out it is a good idea to spend the night before your departure at Grundy Lake Provincial Park, just a few kilometers down the road from the put-in at Key River. By spending the night at Grundy Lake Provincial Park, you can

*Still water in the south interior of the Bustard Islands.*

take a full day to paddle down the Key River and out to a campsite on the way to the Bustards. There are a few places to camp on the north side of the Key River, but the south side is part of the Henvey Inlet Indian Reserve and is off-limits to camping. We strongly recommend staying at the park and taking a complete day to paddle the 18 to 20 kilometers that get you out to the first good camping on the south end of Dokis Island or on the mainland north of Dead Island.

Dead Island is home to a Native burial site and should be respected just as you would any churchyard or cemetery. Please show your respect by finding another place to spend the night. The graves on this island were both in the ground under piles of stones and on tree platforms. These graves were raided for an exhibition at the World's Fair in Chicago. None of the stolen grave goods or bodies were ever returned to the island.

As you paddle out of the mouth of the Key River into the village of Key Harbour you will see many wooden pilings on the northern shore extending out into the bay for several hundred meters. These are remains of a large shipping dock that at various times shipped coal and steel. From the mouth of the river it is a straight shot west to the Dead Island Channel, which brings you within sight of the Bustards.

From the Dead Island Channel to the Bustard Islands is 5 kilometers in a straight line, but that is not always the best way to paddle to them. It is far safer and much less work to thread your way through the Shirt Tails or the Outer Fox Islands and then paddle across to the Bustards. Once on the Bustards, find a secluded campsite and set up for the next couple of days.

When you are choosing a site, take the ever-changing weather into account. Friends of ours set up one gloriously calm evening on a rock spit facing the sunset. A couple of hours after they went to sleep they woke to the wind howling around their tent and the sound of their kayaks being blown across the rocks. They spent the rest of a long, wet, miserable night making sure their kayaks stayed with them and keeping their tent anchored to terra firma. If you are planning to stay on the Bustards for a couple of days, which is the minimum time needed to explore them, make sure that your tent will be sheltered from the prevailing westerlies.

As you paddle in from the east, you won't be able to see the lighthouse and range lights on the Bustard Rocks to the west of the Bustards. These are worth a visit on your first full day exploring the islands. Look for one lighthouse and two range towers on the Bustard Rocks to the west of the main islands of the Bustards group. These towers have been

*Down one of the many inlets of the Bustard Islands.*

here since 1875, when they were first commissioned. They are now maintained by the Coast Guard, but used to be manned by lighthouse personnel who lived on the islands with their families for the spring, summer and fall. The lighthouse keeper longest in residence was also the last. Thomas William Flynn took care of the light from 1928 until 1951, when the lights were automated.

After exploring the Bustard Rocks and the lighthouses, you still have a huge area to explore for the next day or two. The Bustards are made up of 559 rocky islands ranging in size from the large Tanvat Island to tiny shoals with a rock in the middle. It is well worth your while to spend a day kayaking the many channels between these islands. The south side of the islands is much more rugged and wild than the more sheltered north side. We have seen lots of mink, turtles and herons on the south side, and there are the remains of crayfish on every little point, evidence of where local furry or feathered residents have had lunch. At some locations on the shore of Tanvat Island, there are swirl holes, kettles formed

*Lighthouses on the Bustards.*

by rocks that swirled around in glacial melt-off, grinding down the softer rock underneath. Even when the winds out on the open bay are howling, it is possible to paddle through this network of channels and bays on almost perfectly calm water.

After a couple of days spent discovering the Bustards it is time to head back to Key River. Retrace your route back to the river and pray for favorable winds. With a good stiff wind behind you it is possible to surf and sail all the way to the mouth of the river. Stop on either Dokis Island or on the mainland across from Dead Island for your last night. By doing this, you have all of the last day to paddle up the Key River and can slowly adjust to being back around lots of people. There are a few places to camp on the north shore of the Key River, but the south shore is Native land and should be treated as private land. Please respect their privacy. It will take a bit longer to paddle up the river due to the current, but it is not normally a strenuous paddle.

## ACCESS:

Marina put-in just north of the bridge on Highway 69 over the Key River. The marina charges a small fee for parking and can also arrange for boat shuttle service out onto Georgian Bay.
Key Marine Resort, Gil Gariup, RR 1 Britt, Ontario, P0G 1A0
705-383-2422 fax 705-383-2282

## ALTERNATE ACCESS:

It is also possible to reach the Bustards from Hartley Bay on the French River. See the Voyager Route, Section 1.4, for details.

## KAYAK AND GEAR RENTALS:

White Squall RR 1 Nobel, Ontario, P0G 1G0
705-324-5324 or 705-746-4936 fax 705-342-1975
www.zeuter.com/squall/

## MAPS:

1:50,000, Topographic Maps, Key Harbour 41 H/15

## CHARTS:

Small Craft Charts, 2204

## FEES:

Small fee for parking at Key Marine Resort. Camping at Grundy Lake Provincial Park costs $19.75/night.

## RADIO STATION FOR MARINE REPORT:

88.9, but it is very weak at this range.

## SPECIAL CONSIDERATIONS:

The Bustards are isolated from the mainland by wide channels that can be impassable with high winds. If the wind is strong when you leave the Dead Island Channel it might be wise to reroute your trip into the Outer Fox Islands where it is possible to stay in more sheltered areas.

## DIFFICULTY:

Intermediate to advanced depending on the weather conditions.

## TRIP LENGTH:

6 to 8 days

## POSSIBLE EXTENSIONS:

You can spend a great deal of time exploring the hundreds of islands along the many outlets of the French River and the Outer Foxes: see Section 1.5.

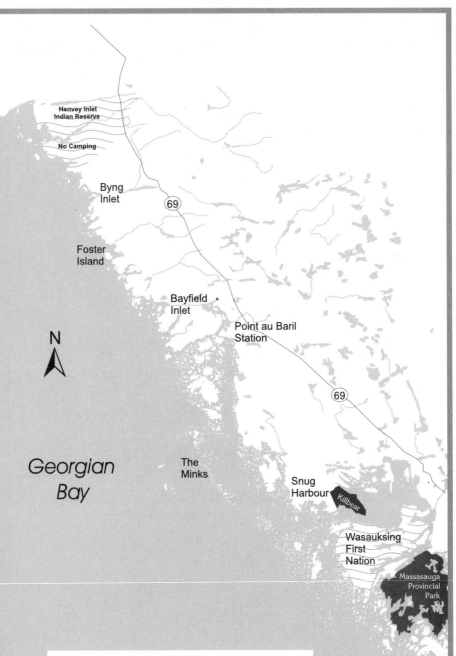

Henvey Inlet
Indian Reserve

No Camping

Byng
Inlet

(69)

Foster
Island

Bayfield
Inlet

Point au Baril
Station

N

(69)

Georgian
Bay

The
Minks

Snug
Harbour

Killbear

Wasauksing
First
Nation

Massasauga
Provincial
Park

Section 2
The Eastern Shore

# THE EASTERN SHORE 2.0

The eastern shoreline of Georgian Bay is dotted with thousands of islands and edged with deep inlets and coves. This rugged, rough coast is home to the 30,000 Islands, which actually number closer to 60,000 islands. Travel by water was the only way to access most of this coast until the railroad pushed through near the shoreline around the turn of the century. Many communities on this coast have only had road access since the 1950s. Because of its rugged beauty, the eastern shore has been a resort and cottage destination for many years, but with the exception of the southern edge, most of the land and water along this coast seems as wild as it was when the Native plied these waters in birch-bark canoes. There are fewer people living along this shore now than there were at the height of the lumber boom in the early 1900s.

The greatest number of kayak routes on Georgian Bay are found along this shore. This is due partly to the excellent access possible from Highway 69, but mainly because of the topography, which lends itself so well to sea-kayaking.

*Mammals such as this mink are often seen looking for food late in the afternoons. They love to play and are very curious.*

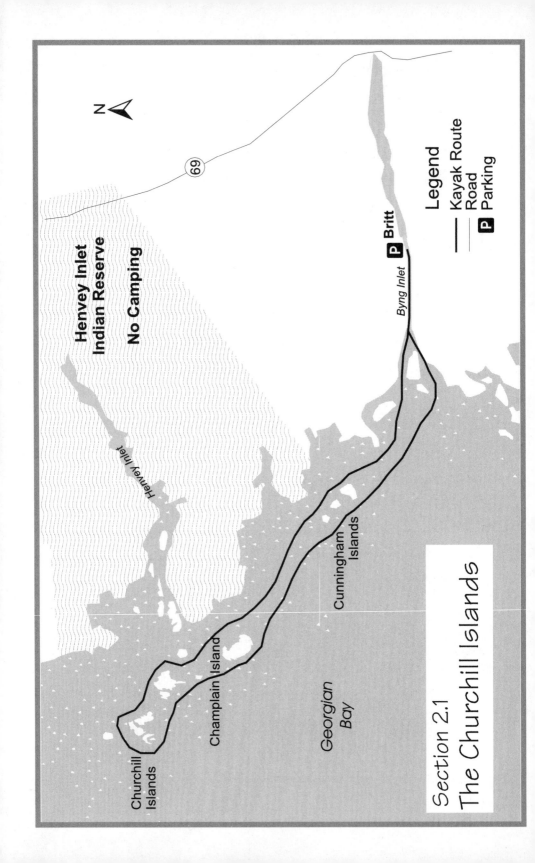

Section 2.1
The Churchill Islands

# THE CHURCHILL ISLANDS 2.1

The Churchill Islands lie off the coast of Georgian Bay at the mouth of the Henvey Inlet, halfway between Byng Inlet and Key River. The entire mainland shore in this area is part of the Henvey Inlet Indian Reserve and as such has very few cottages and is off-limits to camping. Several years ago, the Churchill Islands suffered a forest fire that left many scars on the islands. The tall, blackened tree trunks stand like sentinels guarding against another fire. The fire was not totally devastating and much of the land on the islands remained untouched. A trip to the Churchill Islands is generally a trip into solitude.

Britt is the best place to use as a departure point for this trip. We normally recommend that people use the services provided at Georgian Bay Cottages. There is a small fee to launch and leave a car parked here, and there is an excellent beach to launch from. It is also possible to camp here the night before or after your kayak trip if you need to travel long distances to get to Britt. From the beach at the campground, it is a few short kilometers to the open waters of Georgian Bay just past Lamondin Point. There are a couple of excellent camping spots here as well as on

*View from Lamondin Point at Byng Inlet.*

the smaller surrounding islands. Most kayakers elect to spend their first night either here or on the Cunningham Islands. To get to the Cunningham Islands, turn northwest after you pass Lamondin Point and paddle past Lombriere Island. Cunningham Island will be directly in front of you. A couple of cottages are located on these islands, so be sure not to infringe on their privacy if you do plan to stay here. Large numbers of mink inhabit these islands and you will likely see a few if you happen to be paddling through in the late afternoon.

It is quite a long paddle from this group of islands to Champlain Island, which is the southernmost island in the Churchill Islands. The western side of Champlain Island is quite deserted and has many wonderful sites from which to watch the sunset over Georgian Bay. The pink granite rocks here are heavily veined with softer, black rock and the combination of these two rock types makes for a fascinating place to hike around and explore. Continuing on a northerly course, past Champlain Island, will take you through a delightful playground of rocks, small islands and shoals. Because of the numerous unmarked shoals in this area, motorboat traffic is primarily limited to the main channel, which leaves the rest of the area to kayakers. Rogers Island and the surrounding islands are home to one of the last commercial fishermen on Georgian Bay. The small cottage that he and his wife live in is one of the few buildings on these islands; the rest of the islands are as wild as they were a hundred years ago.

The actual Churchill Islands are northwest of Rogers Island across a rock-studded passage. Entering the channel, which runs north through the islands, is much like paddling back in time. The sense of isolation here is almost overwhelming. The stark trunks of windswept trees silhouetted against the sky and mirrored in the still water in this channel can make you feel as if a party of Natives or courier de bois in birchbark canoes may paddle around the corner and out of the past at any minute. The rugged terrain on the Churchill Islands makes camping sites a little more difficult to find, but there are a few real gems here.

It is possible to set up a base on the Churchill Islands from which you can explore the many islands surrounding Solitary Rock and One Tree Island, directly west of the Churchill Islands. A superb daytrip can be made by paddling out through these islands and then swinging north through the shoals around Murray Rock to Dead Island. Dead Island is home to a Native burial ground and should be treated with the respect

*Fall paddling near Byng Inlet.*

any burial or religious site deserves. From Dead Island, follow a course eastward to Bigsby Island and then turn south following the chain of islands back to the Churchill Islands and your campsite.

Another excellent daytrip from your site on the Churchill Islands is a trip up into Henvey Inlet. The islands at the mouth of the inlet shield the entrance from most westerly winds, so this is a great place to go on windy days. Once on the inlet, you will feel as if you are traveling on a long lake rather than on the big open waters of Georgian Bay. All of the mainland on both sides of Henvey Inlet is part of Henvey Inlet Indian Reserve and is private land. Please respect their rights as property owners and do not trespass.

Returning from the Churchill Islands to Britt and your waiting vehicle is just a reversal of the steps taken to get out to the islands. It is possible, however, to paddle back within 200 meters of your outgoing route and still have it seem as if you have never been there before. By taking the

*The sculpted channels of Cunningham Island.*

opposite side of the islands from your original route, you will see more interesting country and not feel as if you are retracing your steps.

For an interesting side trip on your return to Britt, paddle the mainland shore of Black Bay across from Cunningham Island. The stark bare granite islands to the west contrast sharply with the swampy, verdant mainland. The marshy area along this shore is home to many different types of waterfowl and is a birdwatcher's paradise. Be forewarned, however, that it is also a mosquito's paradise and any exposed flesh will be attacked after dusk. The bugs seem to be fine during the daytime, but night brings the swarms out by the millions. In the fall, the colors here are fantastic, and if you are lucky, you will be here at the same time as the birds are congregating to prepare for the long flight south. Another bonus to fall paddling here: there are no bugs!

Once you have rounded Lamondin Point you are almost finished the physical part of the Churchill Islands experience, but the haunting solitude you felt while paddling through the myriad of islands will last long after you return home.

# FOSTER ISLAND 2.2

The section of coast stretching south from the mouth of Byng Inlet to the Alexander Passage leading into Bayfield Inlet is one of the most untouched and pristine places on Georgian Bay. The flat, shelving rocks and the numerous shoals that they create have ensured that those traveling in larger boats stay well clear of this area. For sea kayaks, however, this is a wonderful place to paddle. There are spots even too shallow for a kayak, but a paddling path can always be found through the rocks and shoals, and the camping in this area is superb. The same flat rock shelves that make this area so dangerous for boats also make wonderful tent sites when elevated above the waterline. Foster Island is a large island located about 8 kilometers south of the mouth of Byng Inlet. All access to cottages or lodges in this area is by water either from Byng Inlet or Bayfield Inlet, so the cottages out here tend to be smaller and less obtrusive than in other, more accessible parts of the bay. There is one large, white

*Paddling off the flat shores of Foster Island.*

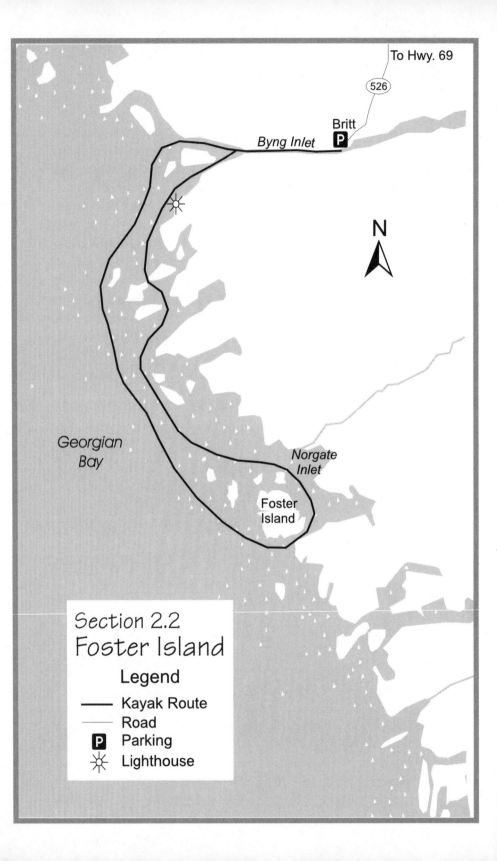

To Hwy. 69

526

Britt

Byng Inlet

N

Georgian
Bay

Norgate
Inlet

Foster
Island

Section 2.2
Foster Island

Legend
—— Kayak Route
—— Road
P  Parking
☀ Lighthouse

clapboard lodge on a small island just south of Foster Island, but very few cottages are even visible for most of this trip.

You have a choice of two departure and return points for this trip: Britt on the north side of the inlet or Byng Inlet on the south side of the water.

Byng Inlet was once home to the second-largest sawmill in Canada, built in 1902 by the Holland and Graves Lumber Company. The mill was shut down in 1927, when the timber in the area was exhausted. There were two mills on the northern side of the river as well and one on Mill Island in the center of the river. Hundreds of pilings in the river are all that remain of the timber industry now. The railroad arrived in 1908 and ensured the continued existence of Britt, though Byng Inlet slowly shrunk to a shell of its former self. The tourist trade and boaters of all types have revived business somewhat in these two communities, along with tankers shipping oil into Britt for distribution by rail eastward.

On the north shore, almost at the end of the road through Britt, is a small campground called Georgian Bay Cottages. It has a small beach for launching and offers parking for a small fee. It is also possible to put in at the government dock in Britt or on the south side of the river in Byng Inlet. Wherever you put in, you face a paddle down the inlet for several kilometers before you will see Gereaux Island Light Station signaling the spot for you to turn south.

The current lighthouse on Gereaux Island was built in 1880 and was manned up until 1989, when it became fully automated. The buildings that remain are used as a rescue station for the Coast Guard and are regularly maintained as such. There are several good camping spots on the southern side of Gereaux Island as well as on neighboring islands. This is an excellent spot to spend your first night. From your campsite, head south through the shoals and banks that dot this coast. If the waves are running high from the west, there is a slightly more sheltered route leading down to Burrits Bay. From Burrits Bay, it is possible to wind your way south through narrow channels between the two larger islands lying alongside the mainland. If the waves are not rough, the paddle through the rocks and shelving banks along the edge of the bay is quite delightful, with huge slabs of glacier-polished rock rising close to the surface under your kayak. There are many colored veins of rock running through these slabs like bolts of lightning frozen in the darker mass of granite.

*Top: Rugged rocks near Foster Island.*
*Below: One of the smaller mysteries of Georgian Bay.*

Norgate Inlet cuts through these shoals and reaches into the mainland to terminate in Kenerick Bay. The islands on the south side of Norgate Inlet are a group of islands clinging to the north side of Foster Island. As you head south between these islands you will end up on the eastern shore of Foster Island. The passage appears to end among the many small islands jumbled together here, but a sheltered passage does exist and will take you back out to Georgian Bay around the southern side of Foster Island. To your south as you move into the bay you will see Head Island and Inside Head Island. These are private islands, but there is plenty of camping along the shores of Foster Island or on the mainland south of Foster Island.

Returning north you will see in the distance a large, white clapboard lodge. This lodge is just north of Foster Island among the Bourchier Islands. A rather unique landmark in this area is an old 1950s car balanced on a rock outside a rundown shack. How this car came to be there, kilometers from the closest road and out on a small island, is one of Georgian Bay's smaller mysteries. Weather permitting, the paddle out to Norgate Rocks and then past Red Rock and McHugh Rock will take you through an area heavily populated with many types of waterbirds. Cormorants and loons are the most predominant, but we have observed merganser ducks, mallard ducks, wood ducks, and buffleheads as well as Canada geese around these rocks. It is best to find a spot to camp before you head back into Byng Inlet because camping spots are quite rare anywhere in the actual inlet. The flat rocks across from McHugh Rock provide many excellent campsites and one of the best sunset views on Georgian Bay.

On your last day paddling back up Byng Inlet, take the time to paddle past the magnificent lodge on Bigwood Island. Flags flying and the grounds immaculate, this place looks like a slice of an earlier time, preserved here in the northern woods. From there continue on to Clark Island, now a provincial boater's day site. This rugged island makes a great spot to pause for lunch before returning to your put-in spot and the long drive home.

*Paddling past Gereaux Lighthouse.*

**ACCESS:**
Highway 69 to 526. Follow the road to Georgian Bay Cottages.

**ALTERNATE ACCESS:**
Byng Inlet, village on south shore of inlet

**KAYAK AND GEAR RENTALS:**
White Squall, RR 1 Nobel, Ontario, P0G 1G0
705-324-5324 or 705-746-4936 fax 705-342-1975
www.zeuter.com/squall/

**MAPS:**
1:50,000, Topographic Maps, Key River 41 H/15

**FEES:**
Parking, launching and camping fees at Georgian Bay Cottages.

**RADIO STATION FOR MARINE REPORT:**
88.9 FM.

**SPECIAL CONSIDERATIONS:**
Wind can stop you from paddling the outer edge of the island.

**DIFFICULTY:**
Novice to intermediate

**TRIP LENGTH:**
4 to 6 days

**POSSIBLE EXTENSIONS:**
Naiscoot River, Churchill Islands, see route descriptions.

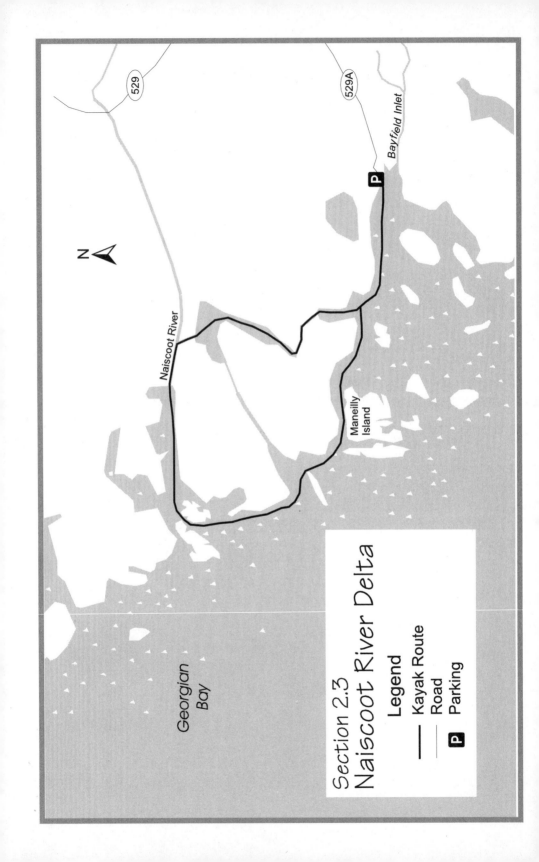

529

529A

Bayfield Inlet

P

N

Naiscoot River

Maneilly Island

Georgian Bay

Section 2.3
Naiscoot River Delta

Legend
— Kayak Route
— Road
P Parking

# NAISCOOT RIVER DELTA 2.3

The Naiscoot River breaks into three distinct channels a few kilometers before it empties into Georgian Bay. From the village of Bayfield Inlet, it is possible to easily access these channels by kayak. Because the water is so shallow in the river channels, there is little boat traffic of any kind. The Naiscoot River delta contains swamps, rocky outcrops and a plethora of wildlife, especially songbirds and muskrat. This short, two- to three-day loop trip passes through narrow, mud-banked river, rocky channels carved by ancient glaciers and the waves, and wide-open vistas of Georgian Bay. Few other areas pack so much diversity into such a small area, an area relatively untouched by cottages or motorboaters. The navigation of motorboats in this area is so tricky that it has given birth to some very colorful names, such as Chicken Liver Channel, to describe the few places that boats can go. Kayakers, however, can go almost anywhere in this area and generally have it all to themselves.

The Naiscoot River delta loop is an ideal fall trip or beginner trip since it is so sheltered for most of the route. Make sure that it is not hunting

*Heading towards the open bay and the only real exposed paddling on the Naiscoot loop.*

season if you are planning to go out in the fall; kayaks don't look much like moose, but it is better to be safe than sorry. We found a shotgun shell in the sand near the fork between the Middle and North Channels. It had not been fired so must have been dropped by an excited hunter. There is ideal habitat for marsh birds here, so we would imagine that the hunting is exceptional. The camping certainly is!

Bayfield Inlet has a government dock and a free parking area right beside the launch ramp. There are no toilet facilities here, however, so be sure to stop somewhere on Highway 69 before you turn off on Highway 529. This paved road leads to the turnoff to Bayfield Inlet (529a), a short drive from the launch area. There is a big marina right beside the government ramp, and on weekends the boat traffic here can be quite intense. Try to stay out of the boat channel as you paddle west out of Bayfield Harbour and into the Alexander Passage. The South Channel of the Naiscoot River empties into Alexander Passage, just 3 kilometers west of the access point. On the north shore, at the end of the road, is the Hangdog Marina. When we paddled by here in late October there was a beautiful wooden sailboat, *Passing Wind*, moored at the dock. The boatbuilder owns the marina and builds beautiful boats here. If you are lucky you may see some of his boats in the water.

Hug the northern shore as you pass the marina and you will come to a bay to your right; cut across the mouth of the bay and tuck in behind Lisnacloon Island. The north side of the island is generally free of boat traffic and there are fewer cottagers visible as you paddle through. Just past the end of the island you will see another bay on your right. This is the entrance to the Naiscoot River South Channel. After threading your kayak through several small islands you will end up on a larger body of water that seems to be a dead end. It is not, and this is where the true magic of the Naiscoot takes over. Once you have found the entrance to the river channel, the course is clear for a kilometer or so until you enter another lake-like body of water.

This is an excellent area to camp, far from the closest cottage and breathtaking in its beauty. Rocks rounded smooth and sinuous from the glaciers flow up out of the water and into the forest. Bonsai-like hemlocks, pine and oak grow out of small cracks in the rocks and cast weird and strange shadows on the water. Over it all is a sky studded with brilliant stars that seem close enough to touch. Listen for the wild cry of the loon echoing across the water. Even on nights when the wind is howling

*Down the Alexander Passage from Bayfield Inlet.*

just a few kilometers away, on the open waters of Georgian Bay, this spot is generally calm and serene. There are many campsites along both sides of this lake and river channel, a few of them little used because they are south of the channel entrance that you came out of and therefore off the main route. If you are looking for a place to spend a couple of nights in solitude, this could be the place for you. Only one note mars the beauty of the area — in the spring and early summer the mosquitoes here are as fierce as any we have encountered anywhere on Georgian Bay.

From this camping Shangri-La, continue northeast to the junction of the South Channel and Middle Channel. Even though this area is marked as being a fair-sized body of water on the topographical maps, most of it is covered with rushes and is impossible to paddle through. But there is a channel through these reeds and rushes, and this must be the muskrat capitol of Georgian Bay. We counted 37 muskrat lodges when we last paddled through here. Muskrats build lodges, much like beavers, but muskrats use rushes instead of branches as their main construction material. These muskrat bungalows look like haystacks in a field, a very wet field with a lot of ducks living in it.

Top: One of the many muskrat lodges at the junction of the Middle and South Channels on the Naiscoot River.
Below: Fall colors and evening light: the view from our campsite on the South Channel of the Naiscoot River.

The channel leading from muskrat town into the Naiscoot River North Channel can be very tricky to find. The actual course of the channel changes every spring as a new one is carved through the silt by the powerful spring runoff. There is a false channel to avoid; it heads almost due north. The correct channel runs east-northeast and is quite shallow in a few spots. On the maps it is shown as a small blue line, and this is the first part of the river in which the current is very noticeable. When you arrive at the Naiscoot River North Channel, turn east and paddle down a river with low mud-banks overhung by oaks and birch. This type of topography, more closely associated with more sheltered interior woodland, is rarely seen while kayaking on Georgian Bay. The large expanse of flat shelving rocks at the mouth of the Naiscoot River creates a place where silt can be deposited and provide a base in which oaks and other deciduous trees can grow. This comparatively rich soil-base allows many plants that are normally only seen further south or further inland to grow here. Keep your eyes open while paddling through this pocket of fragile plants.

The Naiscoot River North Channel opens up into a long and narrow bay stretching out into Georgian Bay. You will know you have reached this area because there are a few cottages tucked into the woods and perched on islands here. Many of the islands have numbers painted on them, for reasons that we have not been able to discover.

Three possible entrances onto Georgian Bay are possible from this channel. The most obvious is to continue straight out the main channel and through the rocks and shoals to the open water beyond. This is best paddled in good weather with little wind and low waves. Because the water is so shallow off this section of coast, the waves can get very steep and confused, which makes paddling in them very difficult. On a clear, calm day this is a beautiful paddle, gliding through channels barely wider than your kayak's hull with the lake bottom clearly visible inches below the surface.

The other two routes out to Georgian Bay are through narrow channels hidden in the islands on the south side of the main channel. The first of these is Chicken Liver Channel, so named for the difficulty of navigating a motorboat through these waters. This delightful channel twists and turns through narrow, boulder-filled passages, to finally empty out into the main bay a kilometer or so south of the main mouth of the Naiscoot River North Channel. This is an excellent route to take if the winds are

*Flat rocks off the shore near Naiscoot River.*

high or if some of the paddlers in your group are not confident about paddling in the bigger waves that can be found beyond the fringe of shoals and rocks guarding this stretch of shoreline. The third route option is a compromise between the main outlet of the Naiscoot River North Channel and Chicken Liver Channel. The entrance to it can be found about a kilometer west of Chicken Liver Channel.

If you are taking three days to paddle this route, the coastline from the outlet of the Main Channel to the small group of islands at the mouth of Alexander Passage offers many excellent camping possibilities. The large, flat rocks stretching back from the shoals along the shore provide tent sites with some of the best sunset views on Georgian Bay. If there is a strong west wind and you are seeking a more sheltered spot, the islands near the mouth of Alexander Passage contain many sheltered and easily accessible sites. Some of these islands are private, however, so be sure to check to make sure there is not a cottage on the other side of that windscreen of cedar trees.

There is a picturesque channel through these islands that allows you to avoid the shoals near the mouth of Alexander Passage. The paddle east on Alexander Passage will take you past cottages both old and new adjacent to each other. Old log buildings and new steel-and-concrete buildings give evidence of the long history of cottages and cottagers in this area. Five kilometers of paddling will bring the Hangdog Marina into view, and just beyond that is your waiting vehicle. Take care on the last kilometer of the channel to avoid the boat channel; boats leaving the marina have a difficult time seeing kayaks as they enter into the main boat channel.

**ACCESS:**
Bayfield Inlet. Follow Highway 69 to Highway 529. Follow it to 529A and signs to Bayfield Inlet. There is also a public dock and launch ramp and public parking beside the ramp.

**INFORMATION:**
White Squall, RR 1 Nobel, Ontario, P0G 1G0
705-324-5324 or 705-746-4936 fax 705-342-1975
www.zeuter.com/squall/

**ALTERNATE ACCESS:**
Nares Inlet, follow signs on Highway 529A

**KAYAK AND GEAR RENTALS:**
White Squall, RR 1 Nobel, Ontario, P0G 1G0
705-324-5324 or 705-746-4936 fax 705-342-1975
www.zeuter.com/squall/

**MAPS:**
1:50,000, Topographic Maps, Parry Sound 41 H/10 (& 41 H/9 if leaving from Nares Inlet)

**CHARTS:**
Small Craft Chart, 2203

**FEES:**
There are no camping fees or parking fees at this time.

**RADIO STATION FOR MARINE REPORT:**
88.9 FM

**SPECIAL CONSIDERATIONS:**
Very buggy in spring and summer. Some hunting activity in late fall.

**DIFFICULTY:**
Novice. Most of the paddle is quite sheltered.

**TRIP LENGTH:**
2 to 3 days

**POSSIBLE EXTENSIONS:**
North up the coast to Foster Island or south through the archipelago of Bayfield Inlet.

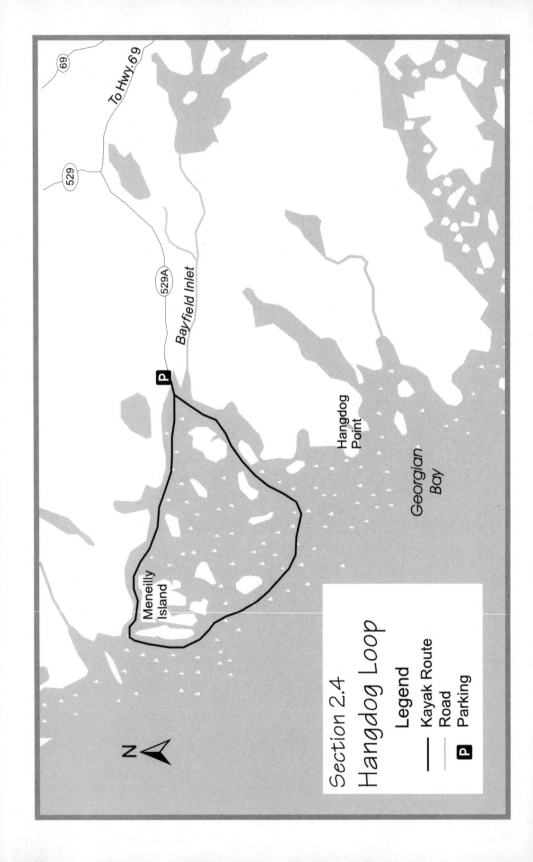

Section 2.4
Hangdog Loop

Legend
—— Kayak Route
—— Road
P Parking

N

To Hwy. 69

69

529

529A

Bayfield Inlet

P

Meneilly
Island

Hangdog
Point

Georgian
Bay

# HANGDOG LOOP 2.4

The place names of the eastern shore of Georgian Bay run the gamut from the commonplace to the very eccentric. Many of the names in use today on Georgian Bay were given to the landforms, channels passages and islands by Lieutenant Henry Wolsey Bayfield between 1819 and 1822 while he was charting Georgian Bay for the British Admiralty. Finding names for the thousands of rocks, islands, shoals, bays, inlets, channels and passages quickly exhausted Bayfield's list of royalty, nobility and even friends in high places. Some islands are named after current events (current, that is, in 1819), girlfriends, ships, shapes, other members of the surveying crew and, last but not least interesting, some islands and channels are named for reasons about which we know very little.

Hangdog Point is one of those names. In this area there is Hangdog Channel, Hangdog Island, Hangdog Point and Hangdog Marina. The marina is named after the landforms, but we do not know why the point, channel and island were named Hangdog. Perhaps a dog was the only survivor of an ill-fated ship. Rocks and shoals on Georgian Bay are often named after boats that have been sunk on them. Whatever the reason for

*Near Hangdog Point.*

*Paddling through the Bayfield Inlet archipelago.*

the name, the Hangdog Loop, through the Bayfield Inlet archipelago and along the shoals edging Georgian Bay, is a superb kayak trip, combining sheltered inner-island paddling with open-water paddling beyond the fringe of shoals stretching along this section of coast.

The Bayfield Inlet archipelago forms a rough triangle bounded on the north by the Alexander Passage, on the east by the mainland, and on the southwest by the wide expanse of Georgian Bay. The Hangdog Channel cuts through the middle of this triangle to the extreme southern tip where it ends at Hangdog Point. There are hundreds of islands large and small in Bayfield Inlet, creating a maze of waterways perfect for exploring in a kayak. Because of the ease of access, the islands closer to the village of Bayfield Inlet are more populated, while the islands along the edge of the open waters of Georgian Bay tend to be much more wild.

The direction in which you paddle around Bayfield Inlet will be largely determined by the winds and weather. In good weather the wind is generally from the northwest, which would favor paddling the outer edge from north to south. Rainy and stormy weather is often accompanied by high winds that can create huge waves, thereby limiting your paddling to island-hopping in the heart of the archipelago. One of the great things about this route is the protection offered by the shelter of the hundreds of islands in Bayfield Inlet. This is one trip that can't be ruined by bad weather, maybe dampened a bit, but not stopped.

Assuming that you will be blessed with good weather, put in at the government launching area, park your vehicle and paddle out of Bayfield Harbour past the Hangdog Marina. Continue along the Alexander Passage for approximately 5 kilometers until you reach the open waters of Georgian Bay. There are a few campsites along the north side of Alexander Passage on Big Burnt Island, but the most spectacular camping in this area is in among the islands reaching out into Georgian Bay, just south of the entrance to Alexander Passage. Meneilly Island, on the south side of Alexander Passage, is completely private and well posted with No Trespassing signs. The islands west of Meneilly Island are almost all Crown land and make a wonderful place to set up a base camp for the next two nights. It is possible to move camp and spend your second night at the south end of Bayfield Inlet near Hangdog Point, but we prefer to spend less time packing and unpacking camp and more time exploring, so we generally recommend using a base camp from which you can explore the Bayfield Inlet archipelago.

The prevailing winds will help push you southeast alongside the shoals and rock gardens reaching out into Georgian Bay. If the waves are too large to comfortably paddle in, it is possible to thread your way through the small islands and reefs out of the big waves. About halfway to Hangdog Point you must cross a channel that offers no protection from the waves rolling in from the bay, but it is only a couple of hundred meters and then you are back into sheltered channels again. This route allows paddlers of different skill levels to paddle close together in very different paddling conditions, one out in the open waters of the bay and one threading through the sheltered channels just a hundred meters away.

The second half of the distance to Hangdog Point is through a granite labyrinth of boulders and wide, almost flat banks rising out of the water for a few meters then slowly returning to the depths. Looked at from a certain angle in the right light, it seems as if the granite rocks are actually moving and flowing north as the water flows over them. Those paddling fiberglass boats and not wanting to scratch their hulls will need to be extra careful in this area, since some of the granite ridges are quite sharp and hide just below the surface.

Hangdog Point marks the end of sheltered paddling possibilities, which makes it a good turning-point for the trip back to your campsite. For the return trip you can meander through the myriad of channels and islands that make up most of Bayfield Inlet. There is direct route north along the Hangdog Channel, which is marked with navigation aids. A good map or chart is invaluable in this area to keep you from getting too far off-track. There are many cottages on these islands, but this does not seem to detract from the feeling of almost wilderness. It is easy to spend two days exploring different parts of Bayfield Inlet and playing in the waves breaking off the shoals along Georgian Bay's shoreline.

When you are ready to head back to the village of Bayfield Inlet, head south of Meneilly Island and weave through the islands eastward toward Gibraltar Island. It is not possible to travel in a straight line in any direction here, but if you work your way east you will end up just south of Gibraltar Island. If you follow a narrow channel between Bayfield Island and Gibraltar Island, you will enter a larger bay that runs north into Bayfield Harbour. Hangdog Marina is just across from the mouth of this bay and the government dock with your waiting vehicle is just a few hundred meters to the east.

ACCESS:
Bayfield Inlet; follow Highway 69 to Highway 529. Follow it to 529A and signs to Bayfield Inlet. There is also a public dock and launch ramp and public parking beside the ramp.

INFORMATION:
White Squall, RR 1 Nobel, Ontario, P0G 1G0
705-324-5324 or 705-746-4936 fax 705-342-1975
www.zeuter.com/squall/

**ALTERNATE ACCESS:**
Nares Inlet, follow signs on Highway 529A

**KAYAK AND GEAR RENTALS:**
White Squall, RR 1 Nobel, Ontario, P0G 1G0
705-324-5324 or 705-746-4936 fax 705-342-1975

**MAPS:**
1:50,000, Topographic Maps, Parry Sound 41 H/10 (& 41 H/9 if leaving from Nares Inlet)

**CHARTS:**
Small Craft Chart 2203

**FEES:**
There are no camping fees or parking fees at this time.

**RADIO STATION FOR MARINE REPORT:**
88.9 FM

**SPECIAL CONSIDERATIONS:**
There are private and public islands all jumbled up together in Bayfield Inlet, so make sure you camp on public land and respect the rights of the private landowners.

**DIFFICULTY:**
Novice to intermediate depending on weather and winds.

**TRIP LENGTH:**
2 to 3 days

**POSSIBLE EXTENSIONS:**
It is possible to paddle into Nares Inlet and end the trip there or continue up the coast toward Foster Island. Could also be combined with the Naiscoot River trip: see route description.

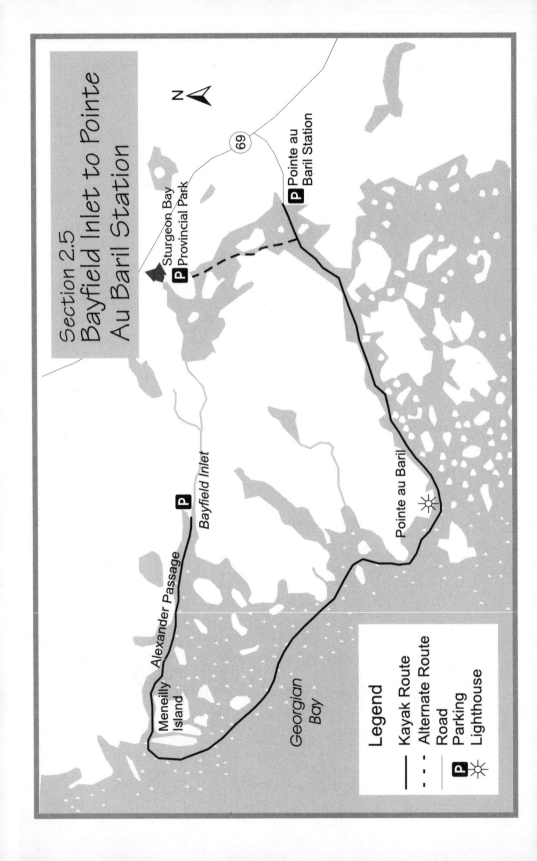

Section 2.5
Bayfield Inlet to Pointe
Au Baril Station

N

69

Sturgeon Bay
Provincial Park

Pointe au
Baril Station

Bayfield Inlet

Alexander Passage

Meneilly
Island

Pointe au Baril

Georgian
Bay

Legend

Kayak Route
Alternate Route
Road
Parking
Lighthouse

# BAYFIELD INLET TO POINTE AU BARIL 2.5

Bayfield Inlet is named after Henry Wolsey Bayfield, an officer in the British Navy who spent 40 years of his life surveying the Great Lakes. As Admiralty Surveyor he spent the years between 1819 and 1822 surveying Georgian Bay. After he had finished surveying the Great Lakes he went on to survey much of the eastern coastline of Canada. He retired as a full admiral, a rank he achieved in 1867, the year Canada became a country. The surveying of Georgian Bay at that time was very difficult work. Two six-oared rowboats or gigs made up the surveying fleet, into which the surveying crew, sailors, gear and food for six weeks were stuffed. They suffered from extremes of weather, poor food, but most of all from the hordes of mosquitoes and blackflies against which they had little defense. Bayfield Inlet contains a beautiful archipelago of islands stretching from the mouth of the Alexander Passage in the north to Hangdog Point in the south. This large triangle of islands offers endless exploring opportunities for kayaking.

If you have two vehicles, it is possible to set up a great trip running through this archipelago, south to the Pointe au Baril Channel and fin-

*The old and possibly haunted Bellevue Hotel at Pointe au Baril.*

*Pointe au Baril Lighthouse. The original barrel on a post was the first light here.*

ishing at the village of Pointe au Baril Station or Sturgeon Bay Provincial Park. Parking is available in the village of Pointe au Baril Station at any of the five marinas located there. Some of the marinas may be able to shuttle you up to Bayfield Inlet to get your car, but be sure to arrange this before you set out from Bayfield Inlet. Hitchhiking back to Bayfield Inlet from Pointe au Baril Station can be very difficult, so do not rely on this method for retrieving your vehicle. You can park your car in the public lot at Bayfield Inlet beside the government dock and launch ramp. This lot can be quite full on weekends, so plan to arrive early to secure a place. Once you have sorted out your vehicle parking and return plans, load up the kayaks and paddle out past two marinas into the Alexander Passage.

As you paddle out this passage toward the open waters of Georgian Bay, you will travel past cottages both old and new. In striking contrast are an old log cabin built of hand-squared logs and, across the channel, a cedar-sided piece of architecture with bubble windows and odd angles. As you paddle further away from the docks at Bayfield Inlet, the cottages decrease in size. Once past the entrance to the south channel of the Naiscoot River, the north shore of the passage is mostly Crown land, and camping spots are plentiful. Don't camp on the southern shores of the passage, however, because all of Meneilly Island is private land. A great spot to camp in this area is in the jumble of islands just to the north of the mouth of the Alexander Passage. These islands are broken up by narrow channels and bays, on the shores of which are wonderful campsites, sheltered from the wind, yet close to the open water of Georgian Bay. For a more exposed campsite, paddle south from the mouth of Alexander Passage and find a spot on one of the many islands on the western edge of Meneilly Island.

As you paddle south through the archipelago, take the time to explore some of the many different tiny channels and passages separating the islands. There is a marked channel, the Hangdog Channel, that threads its way through the middle of the rocks and shoals that take you past Hangdog Point and into Nares Inlet. The stretch of water from Nares Inlet to Pointe au Baril is completely open to the full force of the wind and waves sweeping in off Georgian Bay. If you like paddling in waves you will love this stretch of open water. We have paddled it when it was almost like glass, but there is normally a swell rolling in, and in windy weather the waves can reach two to three meters. This is also a good place to look for a spot to camp for the night. There are very few camping opportunities between the entrance to the Pointe au Baril Channel and Pointe au Baril Station, so it is best to camp before entering the channel.

The last day of paddling will take you past the Pointe au Baril Lighthouse and into the Pointe au Baril Channel. On the islands south of the lighthouse you will see some dilapidated buildings; these are all that remains of the Bellevue Hotel and Resort. The existing building was constructed in 1920 to replace an earlier building destroyed by fire. The original was erected by Samuel Oldfield in 1900 from wood salvaged from a wrecked lumber carrier. There are rumors that the hotel is haunted, but the ghosts are probably getting lonely as it has not been in operation for many, many years. This entire area is still private property, so please do your sightseeing from your kayak.

There is a barrel, not the original, still on a pole marking the entrance to the Pointe au Baril Channel. The original barrel, with part of one side removed and a lamp put in it, was possibly the first light station on Georgian Bay. The original barrel that gave Pointe au Baril its name was thought to have been placed here by voyageurs or courier de bois. One story claims that a group of paddlers found a keg of whisky floating and

*Kayak still-life near Pointe au Baril.*

placed it here to celebrate such a discovery. The question of where this keg of whisky came from when there were very few Europeans in the area has yet to be answered, but it does make a good tale. Whatever the origin of the first barrel, a replacement has been maintained here to this day as a remembrance of that first navigational aid.

Once beyond the lighthouse and the ghost hotel, you will see a provincial boating site on the north shore. There are docks, picnic tables and washrooms here, as well as a large number of boats that are generally moored here. This is a fine place to stop for lunch and is the last good landing spot on public land before the village of Pointe au Baril Station. The 10 kilometers from Pointe au Baril Lighthouse to Pointe au Baril Station along the Pointe au Baril Channel are noteworthy primarily because of the many old cottage holdings. The area around the lighthouse was once the focal point of activity, but the arrival of the railroad changed the focus point to Pointe au Baril Station. Many of these cottages have been here since the turn of the century. Because the railroad came so close to the shore at Pointe au Baril Station, this was one of the first sections to be developed as a cottage and lodge destination. The main hazard to worry about in this area is the boat traffic traveling to and from Pointe au Baril Station to the many cottages to the south and west. Once you are safely landed and unloaded in Pointe au Baril Station, it is a short drive to recover your vehicle at Bayfield Inlet.

Another possible finish to this trip would be to paddle north from the end of the Pointe au Baril Channel to Sturgeon Bay Provincial Park. If you are planning this, be sure to make a reservation with the park office and have arranged to either park your car there or have someone drive you to Bayfield Inlet to retrieve your car. Staying at the park for your last night can act as a nice bridge between the wilderness feeling found on the outer banks and the often hectic life you will return to after the trip.

ACCESS:
Bayfield Inlet; follow Highway 69 to Highway 529. Follow it to 529A and signs to Bayfield Inlet. There is also a public dock and launch ramp and public parking beside the ramp. Pointe au Baril Station is right on Highway 69. Drive west into the village spread out on the shore and find one of the many marinas.

## INFORMATION:
White Squall, RR 1 Nobel, Ontario, P0G 1G0
705-324-5324 or 705-746-4936 fax 705-342-1975
www.zeuter.com/squall/

## ALTERNATE ACCESS:
Nares Inlet, follow signs on Highway 529A. Sturgeon Bay Provincial Park, follow signs from Highway 69 just north of Pointe au Baril Station.

## KAYAK AND GEAR RENTALS:
White Squall, RR 1 Nobel, Ontario, Canada P0G 1G0
705-324-5324 or 705-746-4936 fax 705-342-1975

## MAPS:
1:50,000, Topographic Maps, Parry Sound 41 H/10 (& 41 H/9 if leaving from Nares Inlet)

## CHARTS:
Small Craft Chart, 2203

## FEES:
There are no camping fees or parking fees at Bayfield Inlet, but there are parking fees at Pointe au Baril Station. If you plan on leaving or finishing at Sturgeon Bay Provincial Park contact them at PO Box 271, Pointe au Baril, P0G 1K0, 705-366-2521

## RADIO STATION FOR MARINE REPORT:
88.9 FM

## SPECIAL CONSIDERATIONS:
There are private and public islands all jumbled up together in Bayfield Inlet, so make sure you camp on public land and respect the rights of the private landowners.

## DIFFICULTY:
Novice to intermediate depending on weather and winds.

## TRIP LENGTH:
4 to 6 days

## POSSIBLE EXTENSIONS:
It is possible to leave from Nares Inlet. Could also be combined with the Naiscoot River trip: see Section 2.3.

# FRANKLIN ISLAND 2.6

F ranklin Island is possibly the most popular destination for sea-kayakers on Georgian Bay. There are several reasons for the popularity of Franklin Island, the most important being the ease of access, beautiful scenery and relative wilderness. A long weekend or a few days midweek paddling around the island is a wonderful trip.

Franklin Island has been logged, but it is hard to see much evidence of the old logging operations now. There are a few foundations and log cribs on the eastern side of the island, along with an old motor on the shore and, strangest of all, an old rusty safe half in the water. However, the rest of the island feels quite wild and untouched. There are a few campsites with privy boxes, boxes that can be very hard to find, so if you are at one of these sites you know that you are at one of the more heavily used parts of the island

To get to the Snug Harbour access point, drive on Highway 69 to Highway 559 just north of Parry Sound and follow the signs to Snug Harbour. If you reach Killbear Provincial Park, you missed the turnoff to Snug

*Mist and fog off the shore of Franklin Island.*

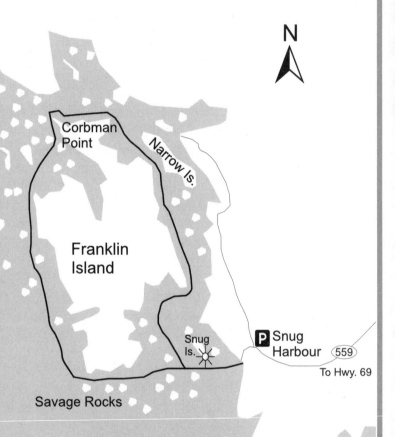

# Section 2.6
# Franklin Island

N

Corbman
Point

Narrow Is.

Franklin
Island

Snug
Is.

P Snug
Harbour  559

To Hwy. 69

Savage Rocks

## Legend
— Kayak Route
— Road
P Parking
☼ Lighthouse

Georgian Bay

Harbour. Park your car at Snug Harbour and load up your kayaks. There are two options for parking at Snug Harbour. There are two free government lots about 200 meters up the road from the launch area or you can park right at Snug Harbour Marine for a small fee. There have been some break-ins at some of the public lots, particularly on long weekends. If you have a vehicle of some value, we would recommend paying the fee to the friendly folks at Snug Harbour Marine for your peace of mind.

Once you pack your kayak and launch, paddle west by the channel markers toward the open water. On your right you will see the Snug Harbour Lighthouse, operated by the Canadian Coast Guard. These wooden lighthouses were built in a flurry of activity in the late 1800s in order to make the bay safer for shipping. They are automatic now but still fulfill the role for which they were originally built. As you paddle past the lighthouse, Franklin Island becomes visible about 2 kilometers away to the northwest. This is a good place to gauge the weather and decide if you should paddle the inside sheltered channel first or head out to the exposed western shore. If it is very windy, the inside channel, the Shebeshekong Channel, would be a wise choice, because the waves tend to build up on the windward side of the island. If the weather is good, leave the cottages behind and paddle across to the island. The southern end of Franklin Island is fractured by several deep inlets that are fascinating to explore. Take some time to paddle into these sheltered narrow bays and find a place on one of the many rocky points or bays to camp for the night.

In the morning, paddle north along the rugged western coast of the Georgian Bay side of the island. On clear days you will be able to see the Mink Islands on the horizon, 5 kilometers west. The western side of Franklin Island is much more isolated and rugged than the eastern side. There are no cottages visible on the southwestern shore, but there are a couple of very good boat anchorages. These can be quite busy on long weekends, with there being more sailboats than powerboats on this side of the island. This can be a wonderful day to explore the small islands and inlets dotting the shore, many of which are covered with wildflowers. We identified seven different types of flowers on one short walk from a lunch spot on this stretch of coastline. Be careful of the surge that builds up in the channels between the shoals if there is a strong west wind. Although these large waves can be exhilarating to paddle and play in, they can also be quite dangerous. If your kayak is swept over a shoal on

*The islands on the western shore of Franklin Island provide shelter from the wind.*

the top of a wave, it is possible that you could be dropped onto the rocks in the trough of the next wave.

As you paddle north along the island, you'll notice there are more smaller islands off-shore, which makes for much more sheltered paddling. There are a number of cottages on these smaller islands, so please respect their privacy. The large bays at the north end of the island are much shallower than the ones further south, so the only boats you will encounter in them are small fishing boats. There is an osprey nest on a pole near the entrance to Corbman Bay. Please do not disturb this beautiful bird; if you camp in one of the shallow bays, the osprey will likely fly over your camp as he spirals around looking for food. We sat and watched him fish this way for at least a hour just before dusk. As you paddle into these bays you will travel through large patches of wild rice. This was a staple food of the Natives in this area and, at the right time of day, you can imagine canoes gliding through the rice as the Natives beat the rice to shake the kernels into the bottom of the canoe.

From the north end of the island, paddle south along the eastern side of the island. Cottages are far more numerous here, as are the motorboats. There are two cottages on a spit of land connected to the main part of Franklin Island, but they are the only buildings on the eastern side of the island. The opposite shore of the channel is dotted with cottages but, except for long weekends and big holidays, there is not too much boat traffic. There is another osprey nest in a bay surrounded by many small rocky islands. You can find many excellent camping spots along the shore here; if you are not in a rush and it is not too busy this is a great place to camp and lounge around.

Once through the narrows between Narrows Island and Frances Point, the Shebeshekong Channel opens up and there are a couple of great swimming spots complete with rocks to jump off and, in the right season, blueberries and raspberries to snack on. About halfway down the side of the island you will see some concrete foundations in the woods — in the bay behind those foundations there are great piles of logs on the bottom and an old safe on the shore. These are the only remains of the logging operations that once were on the island.

Once you reach the end of the channel you will see a large bay opening up to the west. This is a very shallow bay at the north end, and there is a superb beach for swimming at the end of the rocky peninsula that forms the eastern edge of the bay. As you paddle around the bay you will notice several excellent campsites, some with a sandy swimming area and some with a picnic table. Luxuries in the wilderness! These sites are very heavily used, so treat them gently. On long weekends and holidays many of these sites may be used by people camping from motorboats. Further down the bay you will come to Regatta Bay, an official boating site on Franklin Island. On one long weekend we counted 17 boats, mostly powerboats over 25 feet long, moored in this bay. There are a couple of docks and a few picnic tables scattered around as well as two outhouses on this bay.

As you leave Regatta Bay you will come to another bay that is much shallower and generally has no boats in it at all. If you have not been able to find a place to camp for your last night you may want to head up one of the narrow inlets at the southeastern tip of the island. If you follow these far enough you can paddle right across the island with one small portage of about 25 meters. On these small secluded bays there are many campsites that motorboats can not get to. These inlets are also a wonderful place to escape from heavy winds if you are plagued by bad headwinds.

On your last day you can head straight in to Snug Harbour from your campsite or you can spend a relaxing day exploring the bays, and points of the island before you head back into Snug Harbour. From the south end of the island you can see the Snug Harbour Lighthouse, which will guide you back into the harbor.

ACCESS:
Snug Harbour; follow Highway 69 to Highway 559. Follow signs to Snug Harbour. Snug Harbour Marine offers launch spot and parking for $3/day. There is also a public dock and two public parking lots close to the water. Ask the folks at the marina for directions.

INFORMATION:
White Squall, RR 1 Nobel, Ontario, P0G 1G0
705-324-5324 or 705-746-4936 fax 705-342-1975
www.zeuter.com/squall/
or Snug Harbour Marine, RR 1 Nobel, Ontario 705-342-5552

ALTERNATE ACCESS:
Killbear Provincial Park, follow signs on Highway 559

KAYAK AND GEAR RENTALS:
White Squall, RR 1 Nobel, Ontario, P0G 1G0
705-324-5324 or 705-746-4936 fax 705-342-1975
www.zeuter.com/squall/

MAPS:
1:50,000, Topographic Maps, Parry Sound 41 H/8 & 41 H/7

CHARTS:
Small Craft Chart, 2203

FEES:
There are no camping fees, but there is a parking fee ($3/day) if you use the Snug Harbour Marine parking lot. There has been some theft from cars left in the public lots, but it is not common at this time.

RADIO STATION FOR MARINE REPORT:
88.9 FM

## SPECIAL CONSIDERATIONS:
Very exposed to westerly winds. Weather can blow in very quickly.
Always allow at least one wind day in planning your trip.

## DIFFICULTY:
Novice to intermediate. The western side of the island can get large
waves, but the rest of the paddle is quite sheltered.

## TRIP LENGTH:
3 to 6 days

## POSSIBLE EXTENSIONS:
Mink Islands, McCoy Islands. See route descriptions.

*Massasauga rattlesnake sunning itself after a brief rain shower.*

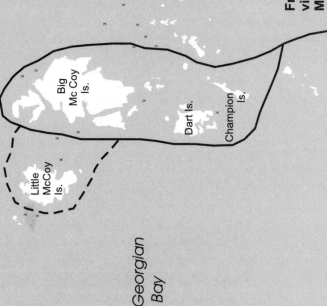

*Section 2.7*
# The McCoy Islands

N

Southwest
Island

Georgian
Bay

Little
McCoy
Is.

Big
Mc Coy
Is.

Dart Is.

Champion
Is.

**From Snug Harbour
via Franklin Island or
Minks Islands
(see sections 2.6 & 2.8)**

## Legend
— Kayak Route
--- Alternate Route
x  Rocks

# THE McCOY ISLANDS 2.7

The McCoy Islands are clustered in a rough circle at the north end of the Mink Islands chain. The two big islands are Big McCoy Island and Little McCoy Island, with a group of smaller islands to the south and another group to the west. Big McCoy Island is public land but Little McCoy Island is private. The owner of Little McCoy was allowing camping, but the current status of the public accessibility of this island is in question. Paddling around the McCoys makes a wonderful three- to four-day trip with the options of easy extensions to the Mink Islands and daytrips to the Limestone Islands.

The McCoys take their name from a trader called McCoy, who was murdered on Big McCoy Island in retribution for his dishonest trading practices. No one was ever brought to justice for this murder, and according to local legend, Mr. McCoy lets out two terrible screams on the eve of his murder, every September full moon. If you are here in September on the night of the full moon, you too may hear the ghost of Mr. McCoy. The history of the McCoys is not limited to this ghost story. There was a fair-sized fishing station on the island and tar marks from the nets can still be seen on rocks on the western side of Big McCoy Island. A great deal of speculation and research suggest that the large, flat rock area on the northern edge of Little McCoy Island was used as a trading center during the fur trade. The large, flat boulders, looking like so many tables, and the hundreds of possible tent sites make this a likely rendezvous for the courier de bois and local Natives.

Camping on these islands is never much of a problem because the predominate rock formations are huge expanses of flat rock that make wonderful campsites. These rocks rise steeply out of the water for about 2 meters, at which point they become perfectly level and flat, stretching off for hundreds of meters in every direction. Please be extremely careful with fire on these islands. Do not have a campfire unless it is absolutely necessary. There have been fires on these islands and at least one of them has been attributed to kayakers.

The most common access point for paddling to the McCoy Islands is Snug Harbour. Unless you get a very early start, you will likely spend your first night on either Franklin Island or Aloma Island in the Minks Island chain. It is also possible to stay at Killbear Provincial Park the first night,

*Heading north from Wallbank Island to the McCoy Islands.*

then paddle north to the McCoys up through the Mink Island chain. If starting at Snug Harbour, you can launch from either the public ramp or the more convenient ramp at Snug Harbour Marine. There are two public lots just down the road, or for $3 per day you can park at Snug Harbour Marine and know that your vehicle will not be bothered while you are out paddling.

Head west out of the harbor and pass the Snug Harbour Lighthouse on your right. From there head straight across to Franklin Island and then decide on which side of the island to paddle up, based on the wind and weather. If the weather report is calling for high winds, it is possible to paddle up the Shebesekong Channel on the east side of Franklin Island, a route that is sheltered from most winds but is also more heavily traveled by motorboats. When blessed by good weather, it is possible to paddle straight across to the Mink Islands, 5 kilometers past the southern tip of Franklin Island. Once at the Mink Islands, you can stop at Warren's Island (Aloma Island — Searle Island on the topographic maps) or continue on to Green Island. Warren welcomes kayakers to his island, and those who stay with him get a chance to meet one of the real characters of Georgian Bay. Staulker Island, Heather Island and Boucher Island are all private, so Green Island is the first public land on which it is legal to camp. This island is heavily used by many kayakers and small boaters, so please tread gently on the land.

From the Mink Islands, continue north past Garland Island and you can see the McCoy Islands in the distance. The stretch of water from Garland Island to Birnie Island at the south end of the McCoy Islands group can be very rough with confused waves breaking over the many shallow shoals and rocks here. Birnie Island is home to a heron rookery and should be given a wide berth so as not to disturb the birds. Champion Island and Dart Island are the next two islands in the McCoy group; there is excellent, if somewhat exposed, camping on Dart Island. The entire top of the island is flat and cut by crevasses and channels. While walking around on this island and the other islands in this area, keep a good lookout for kettles, also known as swirl holes. These indentations in the rock are the result of fast-moving meltwater swirling a hard rock around and around in the same place, grinding a hole down into the softer rock below. Kettles are not limited to flat horizontal rocks; there are a couple of large holes in the rocks on the south side of Big McCoy Island. These larger kettles are used as offering places by the local Native groups in the practice of their religious ceremonies, so please treat them with the respect they deserve.

There are several excellent campsites on Big McCoy that work well as a base from which to explore the islands. Chose your campsite with care: a westward-facing site will give you excellent sunsets but very little wind protection. An east-facing site will be far more sheltered and will not have late afternoon and evening sun but will provide more shade on those hot summer afternoons. You can spend an entire day exploring these islands, both by kayak and on foot. Take the time to get out of your boat and explore inland. There are some tar marks from the linen fishnets that were tarred and then dried in the sun on Big McCoy Island, and the huge, table-like blocks on Little McCoy are worth investigation. A word of warning, though: there is an algae that grows in a thin film over the rocks at the water's edge; it is extremely slippery, so be very careful getting in and out of your kayak. This is also the home territory of the Massasauga rattlesnake, so watch your step when hiking around the islands. These snakes are much more afraid of you than you are of them, but they will strike if frightened or cornered. They are listed as threatened

*Heading north from Raper Island towards the McCoy Islands.*

on the endangered species list, so please do not harm them if you are lucky enough to see one.

Another excellent daytrip from the McCoys is a paddle out to the Limestone Islands and back. The Limestones are a provincial nature reserve and are well worth a visit if you are an experienced paddler. There are 4 kilometers of very open water leading to the Limestone Islands. The waves out there can be easily double what they are on the eastern side of the Mink and McCoy Islands. While we were on the Mink Islands camping, an expert kayaker lost his boat and was lucky to make it back to land safely. The waves on that day had increased from about a meter just before noon to 3 meters an hour later. Do not head out to the Limestones if the weather looks threatening or if you are in any way not confident of your abilities. If you do get to the Limestone Islands you will discover fossils everywhere. Do not plan on staying on the islands because the land is far too fragile to support many people camping here.

The paddle around Hertzberg Island to the northeast of the McCoys makes a prime daytrip or you can make it the first leg of your return to

Snug Harbour. Proceed north from Big McCoy Island for a little over 3 kilometers to the end of the long peninsula that juts northwest from Hertzberg Island. This will take you into Frederic Inlet, which in turn empties into Shawanaga Inlet. If you go north from here, you will come to Pointe au Baril. If you paddle south for several kilometers you will pass the Twin Sisters Islands on you way to the Oak Islands. The Oak Islands are private, but by paddling through the scattering of rocks and islands stretching south from here you will find your way to Franklin Island. The many campsites on Franklin make it a superb spot to spend your last night before returning to Snug Harbour in the morning.

ACCESS:
Snug Harbour; follow Highway 69 to Highway 559. Follow signs to Snug Harbour. Snug Harbour Marine offers launch spot and parking for $3/day. There is a public dock and two public parking lots close to the water. Ask the folks at the marina for directions.

INFORMATION:
White Squall, RR 1 Nobel, Ontario, P0G 1G0
705-324-5324 or 705-746-4936 fax 705-342-1975
www.zeuter.com/squall/
or Snug Harbour Marine, RR 1 Nobel, Ontario 705-342-5552

ALTERNATE ACCESS:
Killbear Provincial Park, follow signs on Highway 559

KAYAK AND GEAR RENTALS:
White Squall, RR 1 Nobel, Ontario, P0G 1G0
705-324-5324 or 705-746-4936 fax 705-342-1975
www.zeuter.com/squall/

MAPS:
1:50,000, Topographic Maps, Parry Sound 41 H/8 & 41 H/7

CHARTS:
Small Craft Chart, 2203

FEES:
There are no camping fees, but there is a parking fee ($3/day) if you use the Snug Harbour Marine parking lot. There have been thefts from cars left in the public lots, but it is not common at this time.

RADIO STATION FOR MARINE REPORT:
88.9 FM

SPECIAL CONSIDERATIONS:
Very exposed to westerly winds. Weather can blow in very quickly. Always allow at least two wind days in trip planning.

DIFFICULTY:
Intermediate to advanced. In bad weather this can be a very difficult trip. It is possible to be windbound for a several days at a time.

TRIP LENGTH:
4 to 6 days or more if the wind picks up.

POSSIBLE EXTENSIONS:
Mink Islands, Limestone Islands.

# THE MINKS 2.8

The Minks are a chain of islands running northwest about 5 kilometers off the coast of Franklin Island. They are full of history and beauty. These islands were the site of a bustling fishing industry until the late 1940s and early 1950s, when over-fishing and spawning-ground destruction ended the fishing industry here. In the heyday of the fishing era, there were over 125 residents on these islands, with hotels, a small floating grocery store and a church. People from Parry Sound used to come out for the dances that were held in the summer months.

There is very little evidence of this activity on the islands today. Most of the buildings that you see today are private cottages. There are a few falling-down shacks left from the fishing village and many iron bars in the rocks remain as testaments to the many docks and mooring stations that once were here. Many of the Mink Islands are private now, including Heather Island, Staulker Island and a few of the smaller islands, and the owners do not welcome kayakers. There is, however, one of the southern islands that is private and the owner does welcome kayakers with open arms. The owner of Aloma Island (Searle Island on the topography map), Warren, has lived on this island every summer since the 1950s, when he bought it. We always stop and see Warren when we are on the Minks or heading out to the Limestone Islands from Snug Harbour. His island is easily identified by the numerous antennas that give it the air of a research or

*View from Aloma (Searle) Island, looking west.*

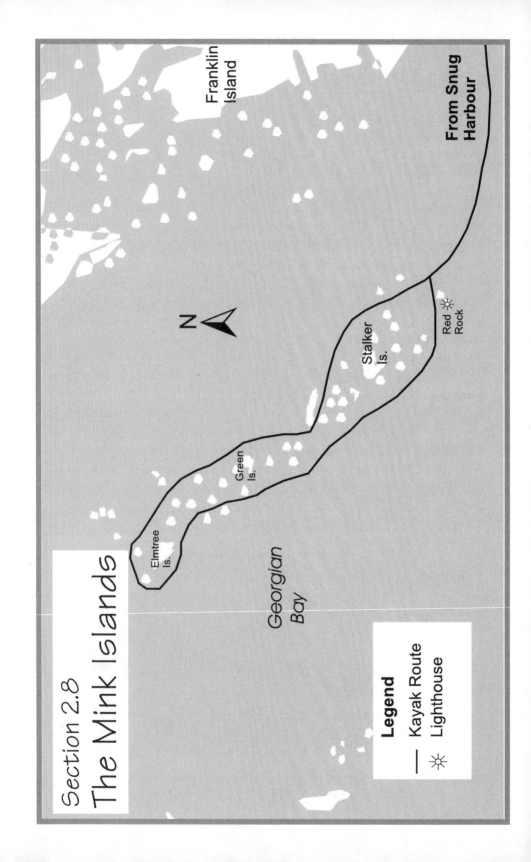

Section 2.8
The Mink Islands

Franklin
Island

From Snug
Harbour

N

Red
Rock

Stalker
Is.

Green
Is.

Elmtree
Is.

Georgian
Bay

**Legend**

— Kayak Route

※ Lighthouse

weather station. Please respect Warren's generosity in allowing people to camp on his island. There is a small toilet in a tiny A-frame on the northwest side of the island. Please use it to reduce our impact on this island.

From the put-in at Snug Harbour, paddle west out past the lighthouse and aim for Red Rock Lighthouse. If the weather is windy, you would be wise to find a spot to camp on the south end of Franklin Island and wait for the wind and waves to subside. It is not uncommon for there to be 2-to-3-meter waves in the stretch of water between the west shore of Franklin Island and the Minks, and there are several shoals to worry about as well. If the water is rough, don't risk it. If all is clear and it is not too late, strike out across the open water. The first landfall that is available for kayakers to camp on is Aloma Isle (Searle on the maps), where Warren will welcome you if he is home. It is possible to paddle direct to Green Island if you have enough time, but you will be missing out on meeting one of the great characters of the bay.

If you do stay at Warren's or on the south end of Franklin Island, take the time the next day to explore the waterways around the islands from Old Tower Island up to Green Island. Old Tower Island is where the first lighthouse was built in 1870. It lasted only a few years before the winter storms of the bay washed it away. A second lighthouse was built on Red Rock Island in 1881, but it only lasted 14 years before it had to be reinforced with a steel cylinder 45 feet in diameter filled with concrete. This lasted until 1911, when the current reinforced-concrete structure was built. In big storms the waves driving in off the bay will break completely over the current building. This lighthouse was manned up until 1977, when it became fully automated.

As you paddle through the islands you will see several cottages and a few old weather-beaten buildings. These older buildings are remnants of the Minks Fishing Station. The cottages indicate that the islands are private, but the water is free to all. As you paddle north toward Green Island, between Boucher Island and Green Island, you will come into an area filled with shoals. If there is a strong west wind this will be an exciting paddle, but the small islands and shoals provide some shelter for the paddle to Green Island. Once on Green Island, find a place to camp and settle in for the night. We recommend that people use Green Island as a base for daytrips exploring the rest of the Minks Fishing Station and as a jumping-off place to head out to the Limestones or as a departure point for the McCoy Islands just to the north.

*Paddling around Green Island, in the Mink Islands.*

While on Green, make an effort to disturb the land as little as is possible. Many people use this island, and if we are all careful, it will remain pristine for a long time. Don't have fires unless it is absolutely necessary; camp on the bare rock where possible and be aware of the wildlife on the island. There are many different types of birds and plants, and if you are fortunate you may see a rattlesnake. This is the home territory of the rare Massasauga rattlesnake and they will sun themselves on the rocks, especially after a rain. As long as you do not disturb them or startle them, they will leave you alone. We know of at least one resident rattlesnake who startled our friend Joan while she was picking blueberries. It is amazing how someone can jump up and sideways and yell all at the same time. Despite the excitement, the snake casually coiled up on the rock and ignored us.

From Green Island there is a wonderful daytrip loop heading up past Raper Island, Wallbank Island, Goodkey Island, Elmtree Island and finally, Garland Island. There are so many channels and little inlets and bays on these islands that it would take more than just one day to explore them all. Get out of the kayak and walk around on the undulating smooth granite, warm underfoot from the sun's rays. This stretch of islands and shoals makes up one of the most starkly beautiful archipelagos on Georgian Bay. Take your time and enjoy it. It is possible to camp on any of these islands as well, but it may be a bit harder to find as sheltered an area as on Green Island.

While out on the Mink Islands, keep a close watch on the weather and, if possible, check the weather forecast on a small radio. The last time we were on the islands we woke up to an almost dead-calm morning in which the Limestone Islands seemed a short paddle away. Weather signs had been shaping up the day before to indicate wind later in the day and the marine forecast predicted high winds in the afternoon. If we had not been aware of the weather, we might have paddled out to the Limestone Islands, in which case we would have ended up spending the next couple of days there. By noon the wind was strong and by 4 p.m. it was impossible to paddle in the waves. While we were there, an experienced kayaker paddling between the Limestone Islands and Green Island dumped and was separated from his kayak and his traveling companions. Fortunately, he was able to make it back to Green Island and reunited with his group, but his kayak had to be rescued by the Ontario Provincial Police. Be very respectful of the power of the bay!

When planning a trip out to the Mink Islands, count on being windbound for at least a day or two. If you are fortunate enough to not be windbound, use the extra time to explore more, take a daytrip to the McCoy Islands, or just master the art of doing nothing. From Green Island back into Snug Harbour is a two- to two-and-a-half-hour paddle with no real breaks. Once you reach the south end of Franklin Island, you will be sheltered from the brunt of the wind. If you know that it is likely to be windy on the last day of a trip to the Mink Islands, paddle over to the coast of Franklin Island to camp the last night so that you are sure of being able to get into Snug Harbour on the last day.

**ACCESS:**
Snug Harbour. Follow Highway 69 to Highway 559. Follow signs to Snug Harbour. Snug Harbour Marine offers launch spot and parking for $3/day. There is also a public dock and two public parking lots close to the water. Ask the folks at the marina for directions.

*Top: Dead calm before the storm looking south from Green Island, Mink Islands.*
*Below: Playing in the waves north of Heather Island, Mink Islands.*

**INFORMATION:**
White Squall, RR 1 Nobel, Ontario, P0G 1G0
705-324-5324 or 705-746-4936 fax 705-342-1975
www.zeuter.com/squall/
or Snug Harbour Marine, RR 1 Nobel, Ontario, 705-342-5552

**ALTERNATE ACCESS:**
Killbear Provincial Park. It is possible to camp at the park your first and last nights. Make reservations.

**KAYAK AND GEAR RENTALS:**
White Squall, RR 1 Nobel, Ontario, Canada P0G 1G0
705-324-5324 or 705-746-4936 fax 705-342-1975
www.zeuter.com/squall/

**MAPS:**
1:50,000, Topographic Maps, Parry Sound 41 H/8 & 41 H/7

**CHARTS:**
Small Craft Chart, 2203

**FEES:**
There are no camping fees, but there is a parking fee ($3/day) if you use the Snug Harbour Marine parking lot. There have been thefts from cars left in the public lots, but it is not common at this time. If you start from Killbear Provincial Park there is a parking and camping fee.

**RADIO STATION FOR MARINE REPORT:**
88.9 FM.

**SPECIAL CONSIDERATIONS:**
Very exposed to westerly winds. Weather can blow in very quickly. Always allow at least two wind days in trip planning.

**DIFFICULTY:**
Intermediate. We have taken novice kayakers out to the Mink Islands, but they were in company with experienced kayakers.

**TRIP LENGTH:**
3 to 5 days

**POSSIBLE EXTENSIONS:**
Limestone Islands, Franklin Islands, McCoy Islands. See route descriptions.

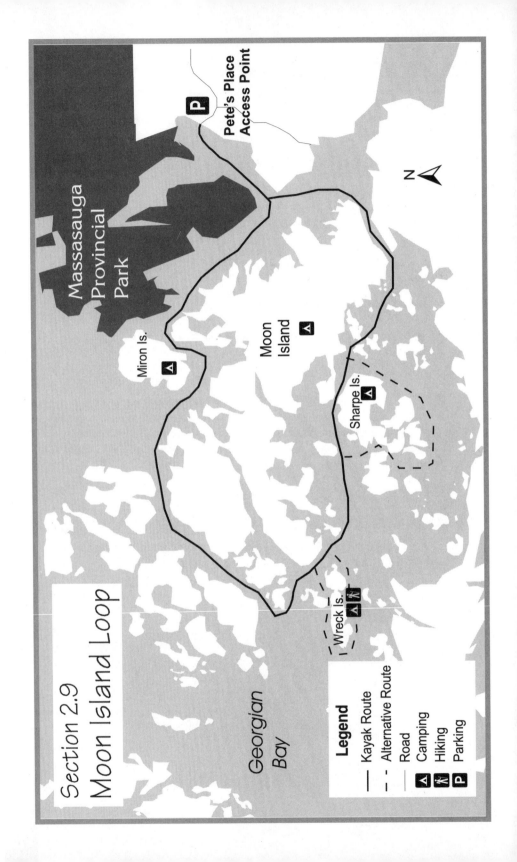

Section 2.9
Moon Island Loop

Pete's Place
Access Point

P

Massasauga
Provincial
Park

N

Miron Is.

Moon
Island

Sharpe Is.

Wreck Is.

Georgian
Bay

**Legend**

Kayak Route
Alternative Route
Road
Camping
Hiking
Parking

# MOON ISLAND LOOP 2.9

Massasauga Provincial Park has many options for short two- or three-day trips. This loop is one of my weekend favorites, though the best time to paddle this route is not on the weekend because of the increase in traffic. But even with greater numbers of people it is still a great weekend trip. Moon Island is the heart of Massasauga Provincial Park. Moon Island was the first protected area in the park, receiving nature reserve status in 1969. There are several small private islands just off the shores of Moon Island, and a few cottages on the island, but they do not take away from the wilderness feel of the area.

All kayaking trips into this area start at Pete's Place Access Point on Blackstone Harbour. There is a launching ramp and parking here, and on weekends there are park staff manning the small booth. They have a great deal of information on the park and surrounding area. It is wise to call ahead and reserve your sites well in advance. This area of the park can be quite busy, and you will be sharing access to these campsites with folks camping from motorboats, as well as canoeists and other kayakers. Because of the numbers of people who want to experience this area, there is a quota system in place that limits the number of peo-

*Squeaking through a tight channel near Sharpe Island.*

*Near Sharpe Island in Massasauga Provincial Park.*

ple using park campsites at all times. The sites on Blackstone Harbour fill up very quickly as do the sites on the southwest corner of Moon Island.

It is possible to break this trip up into either a two- or three-day trip by varying the places at which you camp. The basic route is a circum-navigation of Moon Island, starting and ending at the Pete's Place Access Point dock. By spending the first night on the southern shores of Moon Island, you will be able to spend the entire next day paddling around the island and back into Blackstone Harbour. This is a full day's paddle, so be sure to have a site reserved on Blackstone Harbour for your last night. For a slightly longer trip it might be better to start by spending your first night on Blackstone Harbour, then paddling halfway around Moon Island on your second day. On the third and last day you would then have a leisure-ly paddle back into Blackstone Harbour to the access point. If you do plan to spend your last day on Blackstone Harbour you should take the time to visit Calhoun Lodge.

Calhoun Lodge was built in the 1940s by an American who fell in love with the area. It is now the park work center and is open to visitors in the summer. There is a delightful trail looping through the rugged landscape for 5.5 kilometers to the Baker's Homestead and back to Calhoun Lodge. You will pass the graves of Baker and his son on side of the trail. If you are lucky you will get to talk to one of the rangers at Calhoun Lodge, who can answer your historical and environmental questions about the area.

Your first night will likely be spent on the shores of Captain Allan Strait, or just up the western shore of Moon Island. It is an easy two-hour paddle from the put-in at Pete's Place across Blackstone Harbour, through a narrow channel and south to Captain Allan Strait at the south end of Woods Bay. Woods Bay is an extension of the mouth of the Moon River, which flows into Georgian Bay through Captain Allan Strait. Woods Bay is quite different from Blackstone Harbour because of the many cottages on the shores as well as the large number of float planes at these cottages. Since the park was created, the properties in this area have become very sought after. Many of these cottages have been in the same family for generations, but there is some new building going on, which may change the character of this area over time. For now, it is a bit like paddling back in time, to paddle past these old cottages and to think what it must have been like for the families who used to come here to spend their entire summer. A lucky few families still do spend their summers here in the old family cottage, but most of the folks in these great getaways are weekend visitors just like us.

Entering Captain Allan Strait, you will once more be immersed in country that feels like wilderness. This is a softer side of Georgian Bay than is seen further north. The woods are dominated by oak trees and birds such as kingfishers can be seen at the forest edge. Some of the sites on this channel even have sand beaches. All the sites on this loop have picnic tables and fire pits and some have tent pads, which make camping quite comfortable and easy. Please use the fire pits provided and respect this environment. Even though this area is heavily used, these sites are still quite pristine and it would be nice to keep them that way.

From Captain Allan Strait, turn right and follow the shoreline of Moon Island north past five private islands to an area dotted with many campsites. These sites would be an alternative place to spend your first night. As you paddle further north you will pass through Hennessey Bay and into a constricted passage between Moon Island and Sharpe Island. This is a main motorboat channel, so take extra care to avoid the main channel. It is possible to stay far to the west, where it is too shallow for the large motorboats, and in this way avoid any conflict with them. After

*Campsite near Sharpe Island.*

this channel you will enter a large bay sheltered by Coltman Island to the west. Two of the points ahead of you on Moon Island are private, with large cottages or lodges on them. A great side excursion is exploring Carson Bay and Nightingale Bay. These two bays are home to a profusion of wildlife, particularly bird life. We have seen mink, moose, bear, herons, loons and many different types of songbirds on a single paddle through these bays. This is one area in which Moon Island lives up to its status as a nature reserve.

As you paddle westward around the point framing Nightingale Bay, you will head between Qui-Vive Island and the shore of Moon Island. At this spot there are several cottages and lodges, some of them quite new but most dating from the early years of cottage life. Continue on a long curve hugging the right-hand shore and paddle through the channel between Barnyard Island and Moon Island. On your left you will see a lodge that has been serving fishermen in this area for over 50 years. The fishing is not as good as it once was, but the scenery keeps bringing people back year after year. Once through this channel you will be in Bowery Bay. Keep to the left shore and paddle past both Barnyard and Broad

Islands into another channel, which will take you around the north end of Moon Island. The channel gets very narrow at the tip of the island, and you must share this space with motorboats using the channel marked on the north side of a tiny island, right in the middle of the channel. It is possible to paddle on the south side of this islet and avoid most of the boat traffic. Ahead of you are channel markers that indicate the shortest route around the island, but if you have the time it is possible to paddle around Vanderdasson Island into one of the many overnighting bays located in the park. Anyone who is a sailing or boating fan will appreciate paddling among the many boats that can be found here on most weekends.

If you are planning to spend your last night at the northern end of Moon Island, this overnighting bay and two overnighting bays that are further east are the best spots to camp. Port Rawson Bay to the east of Bear Island and Gilman Bay to the south of Miron Island have several campsites and are just a few hours' paddle from Pete's Place Access Point on Blackstone Harbour. The last few kilometers of paddling south into Woods Bay are dominated by the large numbers of cottages and related boats that dot the eastern shore. The eastern entrance to the channel around Francis Island, which guards the entrance to Woods Bay from the north, is very easy to miss. The opening is only a few meters wide, but it is a nice sheltered paddle through a channel lined with newer cottages on the eastern side and older, decrepit cottages on the western shore. From the north end of Woods Bay, paddle east back through the same passage that took you out of Blackstone Harbour on the day you left. If you are staying on Blackstone Harbour, make sure that your food is well protected from nature's bandits and then head over to Calhoun Lodge to hike the trail to Baker's Homestead. This is a lovely place to end a weekend escape.

ACCESS:
Pete's Place Access Point, Massasauga Provincial Park. Highway 69 to Mactier Road (612). Follow Healey Lake Road for 16.5 kilometers to landing.

KAYAK AND GEAR RENTALS:
White Squall, RR 1 Nobel, Ontario, P0G 1G0
705-324-5324 or 705-746-4936 fax 705-342-1975
www.zeuter.com/squall/

**MAPS:**
1:50,000, Topographic Maps, 41 H/1 & 31 E/4, Massasauga Provincial Park Map.

**CHARTS:**
Small Craft Chart, 2202

**FEES:**
Camping fees are $6/day/person with a maximum of 9 on one site. Reservations are highly recommended, especially in the summer months. If arriving midweek there is often no one available to take fees, so it is best to check with the reservation service first. Reservations are handled through Massasauga Management Company located in Oastler Lake Provincial Park. There is also the Oastler Lake Staff House, which is a lodge that provides a place to stay on the night before your trip ensuring an early start the following day. Fees are $10/night, and space is limited so book ahead. The access number for both the reservations and lodge is 705-378-2401. If you do park at Pete's Place Access Point and do not have a vehicle permit (which is part of your camping permit) you will be ticketed. There is also a limit of one vehicle per site allowed at this parking lot. Additional vehicles must be parked at local marinas. Contact the park for information.
The Massasauga Provincial Park
RR 2 Parry Sound, Ontario, P2A 2W6
705-378-2401

**RADIO STATION FOR MARINE REPORT:**
FM 88.9

**SPECIAL CONSIDERATIONS:**
This area can be quite crowded on weekends throughout the summer. Make reservations.

**DIFFICULTY:**
Novice.

**TRIP LENGTH:**
2 to 3 days

**POSSIBLE EXTENSIONS:**
It is possible to spend a couple of extra days exploring the western side of the park. The trail at Calhoun Lodge to Baker's Homestead is well worth hiking.

# SANS SOUCI LOOP 2.10

The Massasauga Provincial Park is a fairly new park with a long history. The park was originally created in 1969 as a nature reserve on Moon Island. Over the next 20 years the protected area was expanded and in 1989 it received full park status under the Provincial Parks Act. Originally called the Blackstone Harbour Provincial Park, it was expanded in 1993 and renamed Massasauga Provincial Park. It now includes 135 campsites and numerous other facilities, and preserves a unique paddling area. The land that is protected inside the park is surrounded by and sometimes surrounds private cottages. Many of these cottages have been in the same family since the turn of the century, and they are an integral part of this section of Georgian Bay's flavor. This is not a wilderness paddling destination; rather, it is a near wilderness experience just a few hours from Toronto. As you paddle by some of these old cottages, imagine what it was like in the 1920s, when steamers would drop cottagers off and families would spend the entire summer here instead of just the weekends.

*Rock formations on the interpretive trail at Wreck Island.*

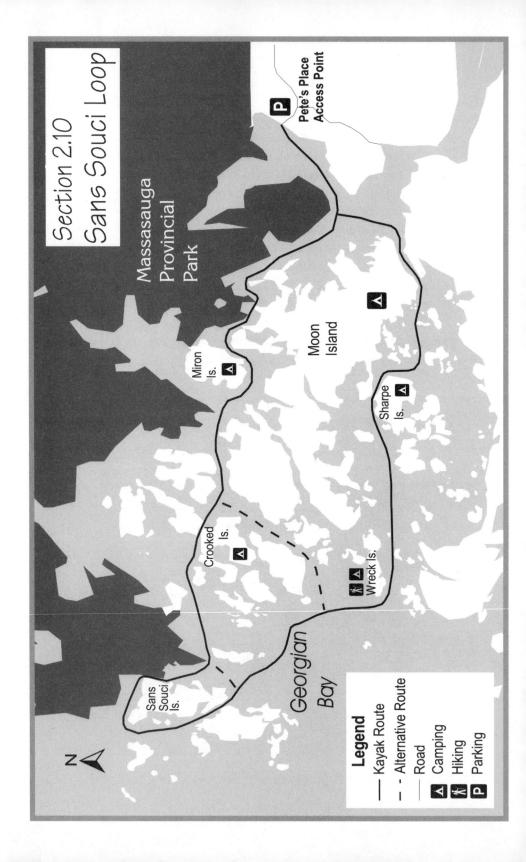

Section 2.10
Sans Souci Loop

Massasauga
Provincial
Park

Pete's Place
**Access Point**

Moon
Island

Miron
Is.

Sharpe
Is.

Crooked
Is.

Wreck Is.

Sans
Souci
Is.

Georgian
Bay

N

**Legend**
— Kayak Route
- - Alternative Route
— Road
🔺 Camping
🚶 Hiking
P Parking

This is an excellent area for a first-time sea-kayaking trip. It is quite sheltered, and if the wind does pick up it is possible to hide behind the many islands to avoid paddling in big waves. We often combine kinds of boats on this trip, taking a couple of sea kayaks and a couple of canoes. It is a great way to introduce canoeists to sea-kayaking.

The best access point for sea-kayaking in Massasauga Provincial Park is Pete's Place Access Point on Blackstone Harbour. There is a launching ramp and parking here, and on weekends there are park staff manning the small booth, which has a great deal of information on the park and the surrounding area. Pick up your permit, pack up the kayaks and paddle out from Blackstone Harbour into Woods Bay. Cut southwest across the bay toward a navigation marker with a large bird's nest on top of it. The opening to Captain Allan Straight is just south of this marker.

You have several options as to where to spend your first night. It all depends on what time you leave the landing at Blackstone Harbour. If you leave late you may wish to spend your first night just across the water from the landing at one of the 12 sites on the harbor. If you have a bit longer to paddle, but not a full day, consider staying somewhere on Captain Allan Straight. Or, if you have a full day to paddle, plan on spending the night on Sharpe Island, Pleasant Island or one of the many sites on the western shores of Moon Island.

Set up camp and prepare to stay at that spot for a couple of nights. The second day out you could either paddle out to Wreck Island and hike the excellent interpretive trail there or, if it is too windy for that, explore the hidden channels of Sharpe Island and Pleasant Island. There are some great rocks for jumping off of on the deep bays of Sharpe Island. The paddle through the marsh leading west out of the main bay of Sharpe Island is quite a contrast to paddling on the open waters of the bay. There are many great blue herons in here, and if you are really quiet and up early enough you may see some beavers. After a day spent exploring, return to your site and get prepared for the long paddle up to the mainland campsites off Spider Bay.

We always try to paddle on the outside of the main boat channel that runs up between Frying Pan Island and San Souci Island. There is far less boat traffic, and the small rocky islands provide a fair amount of shelter from the open waters of Georgian Bay. If there is a strong west wind or if you are traveling with a group that includes both kayaks and canoes, it

*Split rock on the interpretive trail on Wreck Island.*

might be better to paddle the inside passage, however, since the difference in wave action and wind resistance is considerable.

As you paddle north, past cottages both new and old, you will pass Yankanuck Island, home of the Yankanuck Club, which was formed at the turn of the century by a group of Americans and Canadians who spent their summers here. The 1904 building still stands and is still used by the club members. From Yankanuck Island, head through the channel between Copperhead Island and Frying Pan Island. Copperhead Island was home to the Copperhead Hotel, which served patrons from the 1880s until 1962, when the hotel was finally abandoned. It sat vacant for over 20 years and was finally demolished in 1988. All that remains of this once grand hotel are some dock cribs and a summer cottage built out of the old guest house. The island is private, so please respect the current owners and refrain from landing.

You will know that you are in the right channel if you see the large white elephant painted on Jumbo Island. Jumbo Island is named after a boy who grew up on the island. He was a sickly child and the doctors thought that growing up out of the city and in the clean air of Georgian

Bay would be good for him. They were right; he grew up to be a 6-foot, 6-inch giant nicknamed Jumbo.

The western side of Frying Pan Island has a few cottages on it, but it is much wilder than the eastern side, which has a small village, complete with marina and store. The true village of Sans Souci is on Frying Pan Island, not on Sans Souci Island. The Sans Souci Hotel was located on the bay on the southern end of Frying Pan Island, but it was torn down in 1946.

As you paddle north along the shore of the island, notice how the trees are small, stunted and twisted by the constant westerly winds. Many of these trees are extremely old but grow very slowly because of the harsh conditions in which they live. If there is a strong west wind with correspondingly large waves, there are few places to safely land on Frying Pan Island. As you pass the end of Frying Pan Island you have a choice between continuing on the outside of the islands or heading up through the boat channel. It is shorter to paddle northeast though the boat channel to the mouth of Spider Bay, but there is much less boat traffic on the outer sides of the island group just north of Frying Pan Island. These islands have several beautifully constructed cottages on their shores.

Once at the mouth of Spider Bay, paddle to your campsite and set up for the night. Most of the campsites are in Gooseneck Bay, but there are a few others scattered around the shores of Spider Bay. If you are planning to extend your trip by exploring the interior of the park, this would be your access point to Spider Lake. From a small, narrow bay on the northeast shore of Spider Bay there is a short, 130-meter portage into Spider Lake. There are no motors allowed on Spider Lake, so it is quite a different experience from the Georgian Bay part of the park.

From Spider Bay, paddle around the shore of Echo Island into Echo Bay, which is one of the overnighting bays for larger boats in the park. Depending on what time of year and what time of the week, you may see several boats in here or none. As you paddle south through the bay, the water becomes shallower and the channel becomes so narrow that it feels as if you are paddling down a river. The last time we paddled down this channel we saw a bear swim across the channel in front of us. We stopped to look at him climb out of the water and to wait for him to move a respectable distance from the water. He stopped and looked at us over his shoulder, shook his head and charged off into the trees. As the sound

*Top: Playing in the big waves off of Frying Pan Island.*
*Below: A beautiful day to explore the shore of Wreck Island,*
*Massasauga Provincial Park.*

*Evening light near the campsite on Wreck Island.*

of him crashing through the underbrush died away, we heard a snort on the opposite shore and his partner was sitting there, looking like a large teddy bear watching us watch his friend. We floated slowly by this other bear and he too eventually ambled off into the woods. Needless to say, we didn't do any exploring on foot in this area!

Just when you may be starting to think that the channel is going to end, you will round a corner and see a larger expanse of water. Heading due south out of this bay will put you on a course for Yankanuck Island, which you passed on your way north. If you have the time, spend another night on the southwestern shores on Moon Island or on Sharpe Island. From here it is a simple matter of retracing your route back to Blackstone Harbour and your vehicle at Pete's Place Access Point. If you have time on your way out, take the opportunity to visit the park work center at Calhoun Lodge on Blackstone Harbour. The lodge was built by an American, Joe Calhoun, in the 1940s and now serves as an interpretive center as well as a focus for park activities. It is also the trailhead for the Baker Trail, a 5.5-kilometer hike that highlights the recent history of the park. It is well worth the hike if you have the time.

ACCESS:
Pete's Place Access Point, Massasauga Provincial Park. Highway 69 to Mactier Road (612). Follow Healey Lake Road for 16.5 kilometers to landing.

KAYAK AND GEAR RENTALS:
White Squall, RR 1 Nobel, Ontario, P0G 1G0
705-324-5324 or 705-746-4936 fax 705-342-1975
www.zeuter.com/squall/

MAPS:
1:50,000, Topographic Maps, 41 H/1 & 31 E/4

CHARTS:
Small Craft Chart, 2202

FEES:
Camping fees are $6/day/person with a maximum of 9 on one site. Reservations are highly recommended, especially in the summer months. When arriving midweek, there is often no one available to take fees, so it is best to check with the reservation service first. Reservations are handled through Massasauga Management Company located in Oastler Lake Provincial Park. There is also the Oastler Lake Staff House, a lodge that provides a place to stay on the night before your trip, ensuring an early start the following day. Fees are $10/night, and space is limited so book ahead. The access number for both reservations and the lodge is 705-378-2401. If you do park at the Pete's Place Access Point and do not have a vehicle permit (which is part of your camping permit), you will be ticketed. There is also a limit of one vehicle per site allowed at this parking lot. Additional vehicles must be parked at local marinas. Contact the park for information.
The Massasauga Provincial Park
RR 2 Parry Sound, Ontario, P2A 2W6
705-378-2401

SPECIAL CONSIDERATIONS:
Low-flying float planes on sightseeing trips. This area can be quite crowded on weekends throughout the summer. Make reservations.

DIFFICULTY:
Novice to intermediate. The exposed western side of Wreck Island and Frying Pan Island can get large waves, but the rest of the paddle is quite sheltered.

*Exploring the shore of Wreck Island.*

**TRIP LENGTH:**
4 to 6 days

**POSSIBLE EXTENSIONS:**
It is possible to spend a couple of extra days exploring the northern edge of the park. If the weather is bad and you can reserve the sites, you can do a very short portage (130 meters) into Spider Lake and spend a couple of days exploring the many bays of this area.

*The sunsets on Georgian Bay can be quite spectacular.*

# THE SOUTHERN BAY 3.0

The southern shores of Georgian Bay are far gentler and more pastoral than the rest of the bay. There are long sand beaches, a rarity further north, and easy access from the Toronto area. Along with this gentler landscape comes much greater numbers of people, more development and fewer wilderness areas. Because of the relative closeness of the southern bay to points south this is an excellent area for a beginning paddler or a very busy paddler on a tight schedule. There is considerably more boat traffic in this part of Georgian Bay compared to anywhere else on the bay: motorboats pose the biggest hazard to kayakers in this area.

Because this area was settled earlier than points further north, there are very few places where it is possible to camp. Georgian Bay National Park consists of several islands stretching from the southern bay to the north that do provide a few areas to camp. We have included only one route for this area, but there are several access points for daytrips.

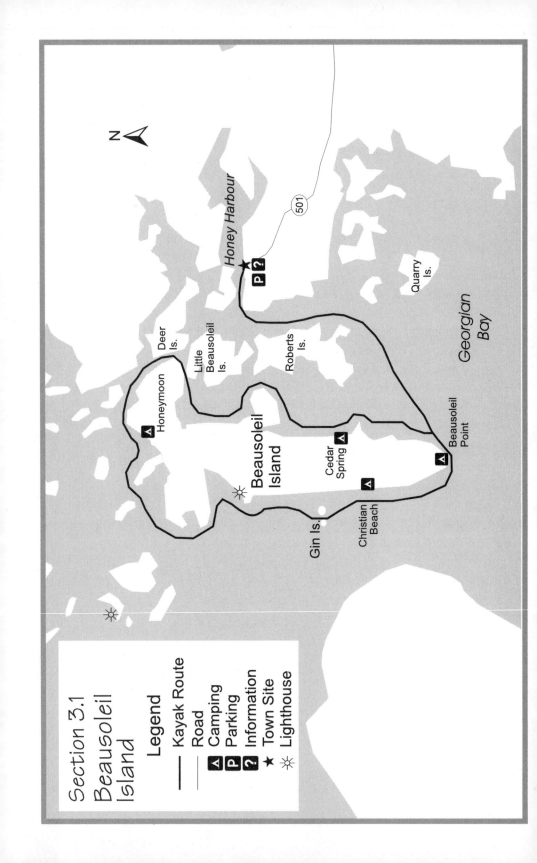

# BEAUSOLEIL ISLAND 3.1

Beausoleil Island lies in the midst of cottage country at the southeastern corner of Georgian Bay. Beausoleil is the largest island of the many holdings of Georgian Bay National Park. There are several campgrounds on the island, making a circumnavigation of the island very easy. This route gives you a chance to experience both the sheltered eastern shore of the island and the more exposed western shore, where waves build and crash onto the rocks and sand. On weekends throughout the summer, especially long weekends, the motorboat traffic out here can be very intense. We would not recommend this as a route for a long weekend trip unless you feel like dodging jet skis and motorboats all weekend. During the week, however, and in the spring and fall this is a great weekend getaway reasonably close to Toronto.

We went to Beausoleil Island in mid-September with two six-year-old girls and a friend from Vancouver who rarely paddles. It was a wonderful trip! Traveling with the two children made us slow down even more than we normally do, and explore the area on a more intimate level. If you can plan your trip to avoid most of the boat traffic, this is a wonder-

*Chocolate ice-cream cone treat from the Picnic Island store in Honey Harbour.*

*Building sandcastles on Christian Beach, Beausoleil Island.*

ful introductory trip to sea-kayaking. The campsites are quite developed with cooking shelters and tent pads. They need to be developed to this extent because they are so heavily used during the summer. There are 14 campgrounds on the islands and one group campground. The group campground is open to small groups and is the only camping spot on the western side of the island. Christian Beach Campground (the group site) and Beausoleil Point Campground are the two most suited to kayak camping. The water off both of these campgrounds is quite shallow, with no dock facilities, which precludes their use by larger motorboats. Both campgrounds have room for a great many tents and they also have a beaches that are excellent for landing and launching. Be careful of the zebra mollusks in the water. These razor-sharp shells can slice open hands and feet very quickly.

Beausoleil Island has two distinct ecologies: the Canadian Shield to the north of the island and St. Lawrence Lowland to the south. There are a number of excellent hiking trails on the island, all of which are accessible from most camping spots. Hiking these trails will give you a greater understanding for this land and is also a great way to spend a windbound or very rainy day. The St. Lawrence Lowland forest of mixed hardwoods becomes jeweled with thousands of shimmering diamonds in a light rain. A word of warning: poison ivy is everywhere alongside the trails and on the edges of the campgrounds. Know how to identify and avoid it!

A trip to Beausoleil Island starts in the small village of Honey Harbour. The main office for Georgian Bay National Park is here, and if you have called to reserve a site you can pick up your permit here. They also have some information pamphlets, but they do not have any good maps of the area. Make sure that you have either charts or maps of the area before you get to Honey Harbour. Parking is available across from the church rectory. There is a small ramp and parking in the shade here for a small fee that goes to the church. When you park, cross the road to the rectory and get an envelope from the front porch for your donation for parking. Parking is also available at some of the marinas, but none are quite so convenient as the church lot.

Leaving this harbor can be quite treacherous because of heavy boat traffic, so be very careful. Once out of the harbor you can either head straight and go to the northern edge of the island or you can head south down the channel to get to the southern tip of the island. We recommend the southern route because there is generally less boat traffic and the campsites on the southern end are not usually as busy. Cedar Springs Campground is the busiest spot on the island, and you would be wise to avoid it unless you are looking for a shower or want to peruse the lineup of motorboats.

You must circle around a chain of islands between Honey Harbour and Beausoleil Island. The largest of these are Roberts Island and Little Beausoleil Island. If you are heading south, be careful that you do not try to cut across too soon, as there is no exit from Dead End Bay. There are a couple of channel markers that will show you where the true end of the island is. A weedy area that is inaccessible to motorboats allows kayaks to take a bit of a shortcut. Beausoleil Island will be visible in front of you a couple of kilometers distant as you round the end of Roberts Island.

Beausoleil Point Campground is at the very southern tip of the island, but it is not visible until you are just offshore. A small gravely beach makes a good landing spot on the eastern side of the point. Make sure that you register and pay your fees as soon as you arrive. There is a self-serve registration station here, and the rangers are quite adamant that everyone must register as soon as they land. There are six sites here and two covered pavilions as well as wood stoves, fire grates and outhouses. Any wood you use here you must bring in yourself or purchase from the rangers. Not exactly roughing it in the bush — but these developments reduce the overall impact that people have on the environment. The national park is currently reviewing their allocation of funds and services, so it remains to be seen how this site will be maintained in the future. Make sure to ask about the status of this site at the park office before you head out of Honey Harbour and when you call to check on site availability before you leave on your trip.

Beausoleil Island is the perfect size for a day paddle all the way around the island. If the weather does not cooperate, the many kilometers of hiking trails ensure that you don't need to spend time sitting around camp. Paddling up the eastern shore, you will pass over a few kilometers of shallow water with a rippled sand bottom. This changes into deeper water crowded with recreational boaters moored to the shore and swimming from their boats. The area around Squaw Rock is often exceptionally busy, but it can be very quiet in the fall, when the water temperature inhibits swimming. Treasure Bay, about halfway up the island, is also generally quite quiet because of shallow water levels.

As you pass the Tonch campgrounds, you will enter a bay bounded by Blueberry Point on the north. Because the water gets deeper here, many of the motorboats speed up, making this the most dangerous stretch of water around the island. As you paddle north, the shoreline changes from beach and maple woods to hemlock and pine forest interspersed with large granite outcroppings. This geological change becomes even more apparent as you paddle through the main channel and come to Frying Pan Bay. The northwestern shores of the island are very rugged with windswept pines and smooth granite rocks rising out of the water in peninsulas and islets. This is the section of the paddle around the island where you may have to deal with some tricky waves. There are several small private islands here that break up the wave patterns and can create some interesting cross-hatch. Once around the last peninsula, the long western coast stretches south to the tip, relieved only by the Gin Islands about halfway down. Because of the shallow waters just of this shore, most motorboats will be well off-shore and you will be able to paddle this stretch in relative peace. After you pass the Gin Islands you will see the beach and eating shelter at the Christian Beach group camp-

*The luxury camping facilities of Beausoleil Point Campground.*

ing area, about halfway between the Gin Islands and the campground on Beausoleil Point.

If you are planning to spend more than three days out here, we would highly recommend hiking some of the many trails on the island. For an all-day hike, it is possible to walk completely around the island mimicking on land the day before's paddle. Carry plenty of water and filter any lake water that you use. It is a welcome change to use your legs rather than your arms after a couple of full days of paddling. While hiking take care not to disturb or step on a rattlesnake. There are several resident rattlers on the island and they are protected here.

It is also possible to visit two other parts of the park, Island 95 and Centennial Island. The motorboat traffic near these islands is very heavy throughout the summer, so be extra careful. The channels that are deep enough for the larger boats that travel through here are not very wide, so the boats have very little leeway in trying to avoid kayaks in the middle of the channel.

The paddle back to Honey Harbour can be enlivened by a visit to the store on Picnic Island for an ice-cream cone. Heather almost fell out of her kayak when she saw the faces of our two six-year-old fellow campers covered in chocolate ice-cream. It is a truly novel way to end off a kayak trip. The picnic island store is a large brown building built right out over the water just a few hundred meters south of the entrance to Honey Harbour. From there it is a short paddle back to the landing and your car.

ACCESS:
Honey Harbour; follow Highway 69 to Muskoka Road 5. This will take you right into Honey Harbour.

KAYAK AND GEAR RENTALS:
White Squall, RR 1 Nobel, Ontario, P0G 1G0
705-324-5324 or 705-746-4936, fax 705-342-1975
www.zeuter.com/squall/
Soul Adventurer, 262 King Street, Midland, Ontario, L4R 3M3
705-526-4201, fax 705-526-7191
E-mail marlin@bootstravel.com
www.bootstravel.com/souladventurertours.html

MAPS:
1:50,000, Topographic Maps, 31 D/13 Penetanguishene.

CHARTS:
Small Craft Charts, 2202

FEES:
Camping fees are currently under revision. Contact Georgian Bay Islands National Park for more information:
Georgian Bay Islands National Park and Bethune Memorial House
Box 28, Honey Harbour, Ontario, P0E 1E0
705-756-2415

RADIO STATION FOR MARINE REPORT:
There are many local stations.

SPECIAL CONSIDERATIONS:
This area can be quite crowded on weekends throughout the summer. Make reservations if traveling with a group.

DIFFICULTY:
Novice.

TRIP LENGTH:
2 to 3 days

# DAYTRIPS ON THE SOUTHERN BAY 3.2

S outhern Georgian Bay has a number of paddling destinations that are excellent places to spend a day in a kayak. Most of these destinations are daytrips primarily due to the lack of camping possibilities and the built-up nature of the surrounding areas. Wasaga Beach, for instance, is home to the world's longest freshwater beach and is perfect for launching and landing a kayak, but it is also extremely crowded in the summer months. Just north of Wasaga Beach are a number of other smaller beaches that make excellent points from which to spend a day paddling along in the surf, but there are no camping facilities near these beaches, which limits their use to day-use only. One possible exception to this is Awenda Provincial Park. This is a marvelous park with an excellent campground and, most important for paddlers, a long coastline. On calmer days, Giant's Tomb, a large island offshore that is also part of Awenda Provincial Park, makes an excellent daytrip from the mainland. On weekends in the summer, motorboats are to be found in large numbers out there so paddle carefully.

Further north, the O'Donnell Point Nature Reserve Provincial Park has many kilometers of shoreline to explore. Reach the park by following Highway 69 to Road 12, also known as the Twelve Mile Bay Road. Follow this to the end and you will be in the park. As the name implies, this is a nature reserve and it has a wide representation of local birds and animals living within its boundaries. This is a perfect daytrip for a nature enthusiast.

On the southern shore of Nottawasaga Bay, the southernmost portion of Georgian Bay, lies the town of Collingwood. It is here that the Niagara Escarpment first meets Georgian Bay, and the steep hills following the shore from Collingwood, past Craigleith, provide a stunning backdrop for a day paddle out of Craigleith Provincial Park. The park is sandwiched between the road, Highway 28, and the water. Although the park is primarily used by folks in large campers, it is possible to camp here and do daytrips from the stone beach in either direction. The harbor at Thornbury also provides access to the water for short paddles east or west along the coast. The waves in this area can build up very quickly and can make landing quite treacherous, so be very aware of the weather and listen to the long-range reports before you head out.

Near the base of the Bruce Peninsula, Owen Sound drives deep into the land. The town of Owen Sound offers a few access points to the water for exploring this deep bay. A real gem for a daytrip can be found north of Owen Sound at Big Bay. This tiny community is home to an excellent government dock and parking lot. From this launching area it is possible to paddle out and around White Cloud Island, Hay Island and Griffiths Island. Griffiths Island is a private island, so please do not land on the island while exploring. Hay Island is home to wild pigs, which are definitely to be avoided. The pigs were left on the island by a farmer who couldn't make a living farming in this harsh environment — and the pigs have flourished on the island ever since. White Cloud Island was home to a small village and even had a school. A few of the buildings remain, but most of the evidence of human habitation has returned to the land.

There are other hidden bays and coves waiting for a kayaker's paddle to break the surface of the water, but these daytrips are the most easily accessible paddling destinations on the southern edge of Georgian Bay.

# THE BRUCE PENINSULA 4.0

The Bruce Peninsula juts north into the heart of Lake Huron, creating Georgian Bay. Without the Bruce Peninsula, Georgian Bay would just be a bulge on the northeastern side of Lake Huron. The dominating geological feature of the Bruce Peninsula is the Niagara Escarpment; its tall, white limestone cliffs line the Georgian Bay side of the peninsula. These cliffs provide a dramatic backdrop to some of the most demanding kayaking on the bay. Deep water, steep shores and extremely changeable weather create an area of unsurpassed beauty and challenge.

For the sea kayaker, the Bruce Peninsula is a wonderland of crystal-clear turquoise water (which is a lot colder than it looks), white cobblestone beaches and vast stretches of wide-open water — with no sheltering islands. Storms can blow in and keep the best paddler wind-bound for days, or the weather can be hot and calm. But even on the calmest days there is generally a swell of a half a meter to a meter running.

North of Cabot Head, all paddlers will be exposed to westerly winds. This is not an area for novice kayakers, as the possibility of having to paddle in increasingly larger waves in wide-open water can make this area a challenge for even seasoned travelers. Despite — and also perhaps because of — these factors, the Bruce Peninsula is a truly magical place to explore by kayak.

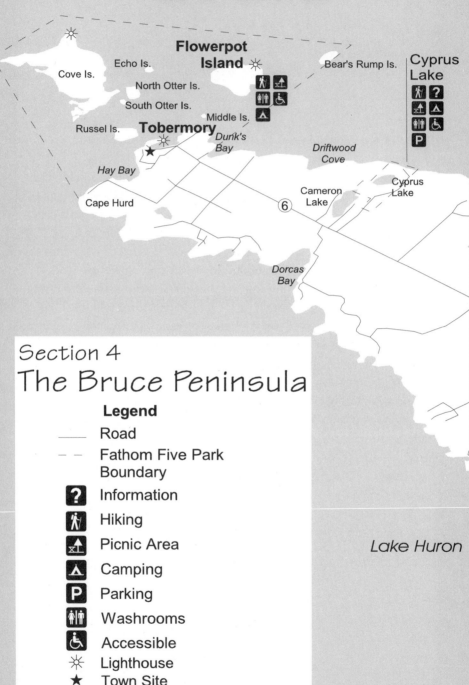

# Fathom Five
## National Marine Park

Cove Is.

Echo Is.

**Flowerpot
Island**

Bear's Rump Is.

**Cyprus
Lake**

North Otter Is.

South Otter Is.

Middle Is.

Russel Is.

**Tobermory**

Dunk's
Bay

Driftwood
Cove

Cyprus
Lake

Hay Bay

Cameron
Lake

Cape Hurd

6

Dorcas
Bay

## Section 4
# The Bruce Peninsula

### Legend

— Road

- - Fathom Five Park
Boundary

**?** Information

**🥾** Hiking

**⛱** Picnic Area

**⛺** Camping

**P** Parking

**🚻** Washrooms

**♿** Accessible

☀ Lighthouse

★ Town Site

*Lake Huron*

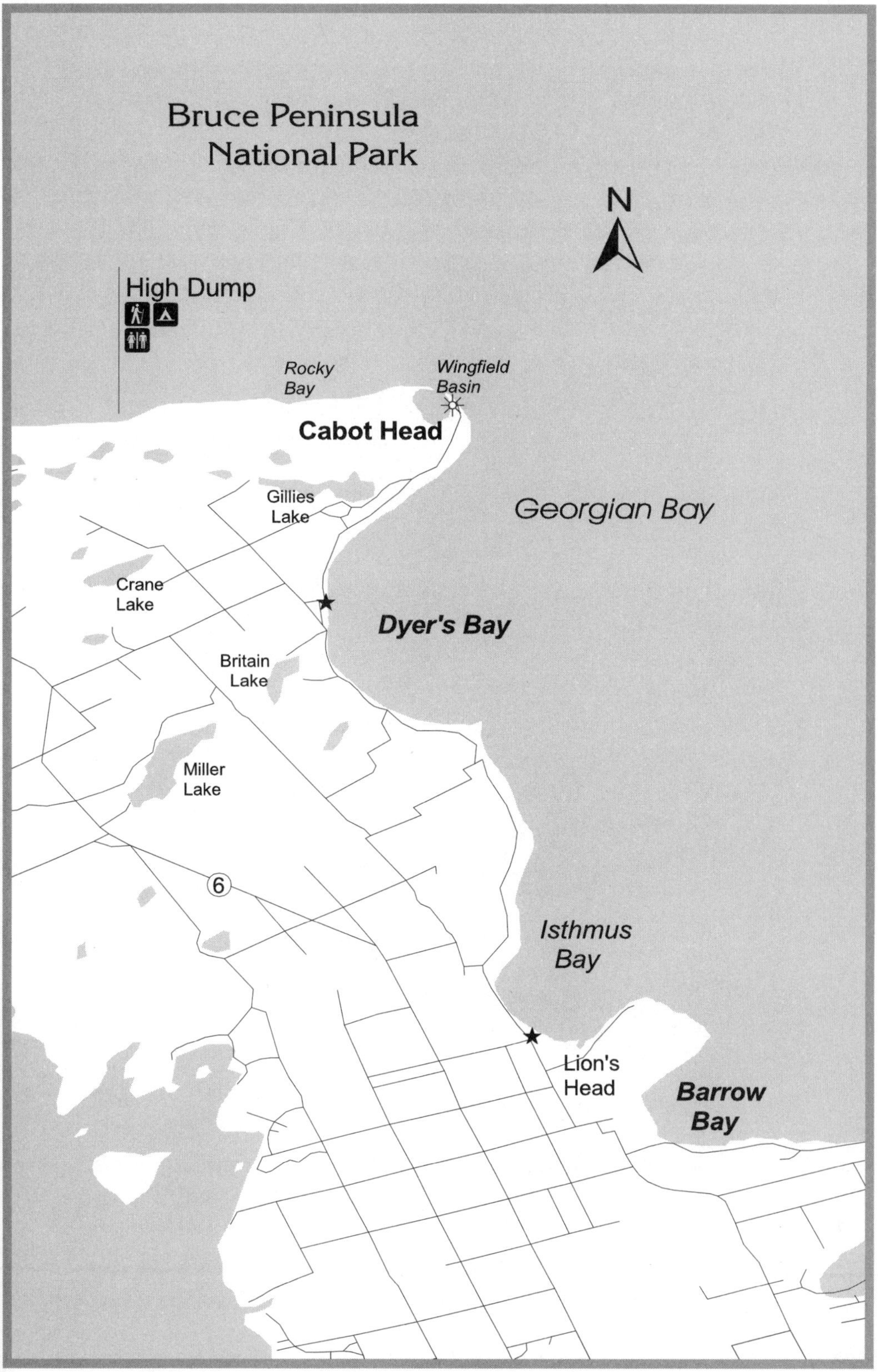

# Bruce Peninsula National Park

N

**High Dump**

*Rocky Bay*

*Wingfield Basin*

**Cabot Head**

Gillies Lake

*Georgian Bay*

Crane Lake

**Dyer's Bay**

Britain Lake

Miller Lake

(6)

*Isthmus Bay*

Lion's Head

**Barrow Bay**

*View of both "flowerpots" on Flowerpot Island.*

# FLOWERPOT ISLAND 4.1

F lowerpot Island is a mystical, magical place balanced between Georgian Bay and Lake Huron. Like all of the kayaking destinations off the Bruce Peninsula, this route demands experience from those paddling it. It is very exposed to strong west and northwest winds, which can keep unwary kayakers windbound on the island for days. It is sometimes possible to get a ride back to Tobermory on the tour boat that calls in at the island, but it may not be possible to take your kayaks on board. You can arrange for shuttle service for you and your boats, to and from Tobermory, but we would only recommend using this service as an evacuation method in case of really foul weather. Part of the special quality of this trip is the paddle out from Tobermory and back into the town. It gives you a taste of real big-water paddling. As you paddle out of Tobermory toward Flowerpot Island, there is empty water stretching as far as the eye can see past the island. To the left is a chain of islands and shoals that extend all the way to Manitoulin Island.

*Flowerpot Island Light Station, where it is possible to stay the night for a donation.*

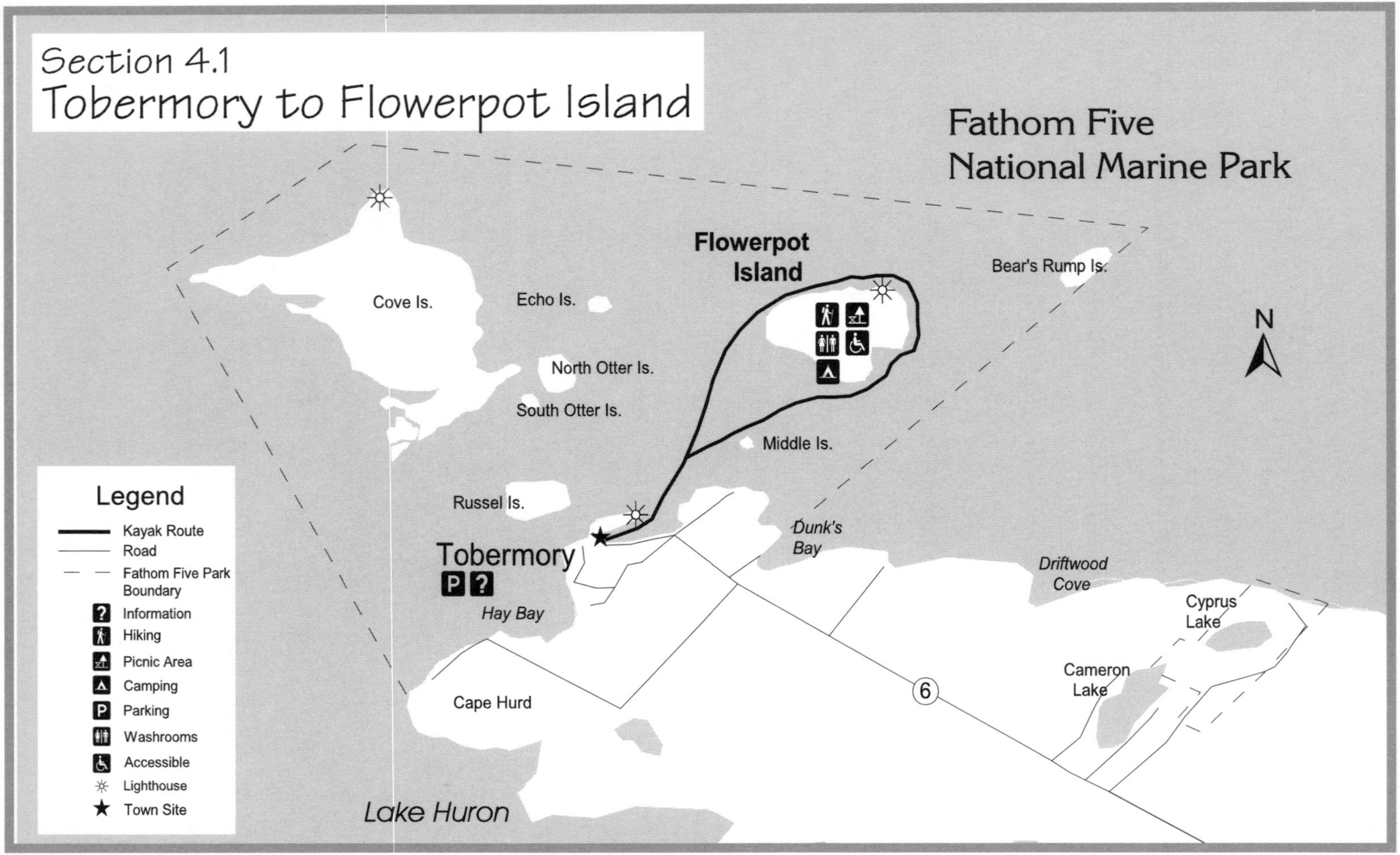

Section 4.1
Tobermory to Flowerpot Island

Fathom Five
National Marine Park

N

Flowerpot
Island

Bear's Rump Is.

Middle Is.

Echo Is.

North Otter Is.

South Otter Is.

Russel Is.

Cove Is.

Tobermory
P ?

Hay Bay

Cape Hurd

Dunk's
Bay

Driftwood
Cove

Cyprus
Lake

Cameron
Lake

6

Lake Huron

Legend

— Kayak Route
— Road
--- Fathom Five Park
   Boundary
? Information
🥾 Hiking
🍴 Picnic Area
⛺ Camping
P Parking
🚻 Washrooms
♿ Accessible
☀ Lighthouse
★ Town Site

Once you arrive in Tobermory, you have a couple of points where you can embark. The easiest is right downtown, at the boat ramp. This ramp will be directly in front of you as you turn off of Highway 6 and into the main square at the end of Little Tub Harbour. This area can be quite busy in the summer with the many people who visit the Bruce Peninsula National Park and the Fathom Five National Marine Park. It is possible to put in here and then park in the large gravel lot just across from the Legion on Legion Road. Or you can park overnight for a small fee at the community center and tourist information center on the right side of Highway 6 as you enter town. Either one is a short, five-minute walk from the harbor. It is also possible to launch from the Tugs, a swimming area along Bay Street. For directions on how to get there, ask at the tourist information building on your way into town.

The harbor called Little Tub, which handles most of the boat traffic at Tobermory, and the larger harbor, Big Tub, just around the corner, have several wrecks on their bottoms. As you paddle out you will see a distinctive red flag with the diagonal white stripe floating in several locations. This flag means divers below, so steer clear of these areas. It is possible to see some of the wrecks simply by paddling over them and looking down through the clear water. There are three wrecks along the shore of Little Tub and more in Big Tub.

From your shipwreck viewing, work your way out through the entrance and into the larger waves that will await you outside. As you leave the harbor, turn right and you will see Flowerpot Island in the distance. This is a good time to do a second weather check to make sure that you can safely make the paddle across. Between you and Flowerpot Island is a smaller island called Middle Island. It is not quite halfway to Flowerpot, but it is close enough to act as a gauge of your progress. Count on at least two hours for this crossing. It is about 6 kilometers in a straight line to the island, but those 6 kilometers have taken me four hours to paddle against a moderate wind. We can't stress enough that you must respect the power of Georgian Bay out here. If the weather looks dicey, don't go out!

Once at the island, you must paddle around to Beachy Cove, where there are six campsites. These campsites are the only place to camp on the island at this time, so call well in advance and make reservations. All the campsites have tent platforms and picnic tables as well as small steel fireboxes. There are composting toilets and a dock for the large boats to

*The smaller of the flowerpots and the first that comes into view when paddling from Beachy Cove.*

moor at. All of this comes with a price tag, of course. There is a self-serve pay station at the end of the camper's dock.

If the campsites are all taken, it is possible to stay at the old lighthouse station. In the summer months the lighthouse is staffed by the volunteer members of the Friends of Flowerpot Island Light Station. They allow sea-kayakers to stay in the old lightkeeper's house for a small donation. Bring a mattress pad and a sleeping bag, but you won't need the tent unless the house is full. If you are planning to stay at the light station, please do not take this service for granted. The buildings and upkeep are all maintained and restored by volunteers, and they can use any help, monetary or otherwise, that you can give them. Through the efforts of these people we are able to better appreciate the history of this area — to say nothing of being able to sleep inside while the rain pelts down outside.

If you are staying at the campground you will not have seen the flowerpots except in the distance as you paddled into Beachy Cove. The best time to explore the two flowerpots is in the early morning or late evening, when the tour boats from the mainland have stopped running. At these times it is sometimes possible to have them to yourself. If you are staying at the light station, then you will have paddled by the flowerpots on your way, but take the time to come back and explore them with fewer people around. It is worth hiking the trail from Beachy Cove to the flowerpots and then on to the lighthouse. The view of the flowerpots from land is not at all like the perspective from the water. Both views are well worth the effort. Although the flowerpots have stood for ages, they are fragile, so treat them with care. Both have been stabilized to keep them from falling over. There used to be three flowerpots, but one fell over in 1903. The flowerpots are in a constant state of decay, indeed they are the result of uneven erosion. As the softer limestone is worn away from under the harder dolomite, the distinctive shape of a flowerpot emerges from the rock.

There is more to see on the island than just the flowerpots. The best way to see the rest of the island is to hike the trails linking the different parts of the island. There are limestone caves on the cliffs above you and a marl bed lake trail that takes you out to the south shore of the island.

If you are lucky you may be able to get on a hike with one of the park's naturalists. These folks know an incredible amount about this area and are ready to share it with you.

Using Flowerpot Island as a base, you may want to paddle over to the closest island, the Bear's Rump. The cliffs on the Bear's Rump have some of the oldest trees in Ontario growing on them. Some of the gnarled and twisted cedars on this cliff are hundreds, even thousands of years old. The harsh environment in which they live has made them grow very slowly. Even though these trees have survived the worst that Georgian Bay can throw at them, they are quite fragile and we must be careful not to disturb them and in the process kill them. On the shore of the Bear's Rump furthest from Flowerpot Island there are large caves high up on the cliff. These caves were made when the water level was much higher than it currently is several thousand years ago. You can easily spend a whole day exploring this lonely island.

The direction of the wind will determine how long it will take you to return to Tobermory when it is time to go home. Some days it is just a short paddle with a light tailwind and some days it is a four-to five-hour slog with water blowing in your face and waves pounding on your bow and chest the whole way. On those days, the lighthouse at Big Tub is an obvious point to aim for, but it seems to take forever to get any bigger. Make sure you are ready for the weather when you leave Flowerpot Island. When you are in Beachy Cove it is hard to tell just how rough it is out past the shelter of the island. If you do have a favorable wind this can be a great place for sailing or flying a parafoil, just make sure you make the turn into the harbor or you could end up sailing across Lake Huron!

Once back in Tobermory, take the time to readjust to the many people. Be very careful on entering and exiting the harbor that you do not get in the way of the *Chee-Cheeman*, the large ferry that travels to Manitoulin Island and back. Paddling beside this behemoth is a scary experience akin to driving a car beside a moving city block. There is generally a great deal of activity in the inner harbor, so keep a sharp eye out for speeding boats.

**ACCESS:**
Tobermory is on the northern tip of the Bruce Peninsula. Tobermory can be reached by driving north on Highway 6 to the end of the road. From the north take Highway 17, the Trans-Canada Highway, and turn south to Manitoulin Island.

## ALTERNATE ACCESS:
You can access this trip from almost any put-in on the north end of the Bruce Peninsula.

## KAYAK AND GEAR RENTALS:
G&S Watersports Ltd. Jay and Sue Harris
PO Box 21, Tobermory, Ontario, Canada N0H 2R0
519-596-2200
Huron Kayak
519-596-2289
E-mail tatour@log.on.ca
www.tobermory.com

## MAPS:
1:50,000, Topographic Maps 41H/5

## FEES:
Campsite fees at Flowerpot Island are $14. There is a fee for parking at the visitor information center, but not at the Legion Road parking lot. If you stay at the light station, count on donating an equal amount of money for your accommodations.

## RADIO STATION FOR MARINE REPORT:
90.7 FM Parks Canada

## SPECIAL CONSIDERATIONS:
In the summer months the campground at Beachy Cove can fill up very quickly. There are only 6 sites so space is quite limited. For reservations call 519-596-2233. The option to stay at the light station helps out with this problem a great deal.

## DIFFICULTY:
Advanced. There is no room for error in this part of Georgian Bay. The wind and waves can build up very quickly and there is nowhere to run for shelter.

## TRIP LENGTH:
3 to 4 days

## POSSIBLE EXTENSIONS:
It is possible to paddle out to Cove Island from Flowerpot Island if the weather is favorable. Currently the only place to camp on Cove Island is at the Cove Island Lighthouse. If you are blessed with very calm weather, the paddle down the Lake Huron side of Cove Island is exceptional. The water is so clear that it feels as if you are flying as you paddle through turquoise-colored water over the cobblestones.

*Cabot Head Lighthouse.*

# CABOT HEAD TO TOBERMORY 4.2

The lighthouse at Cabot Head has been directing shipping for over one hundred years, and even though the light has been replaced by an automated light on a steel tower, the lighthouse still lives on. It is maintained and operated as a museum by the Friends of Cabot Head. These dedicated volunteers have restored the buildings and offer guided and unguided tours of the lighthouse. From a small start in 1993, they now have thousands of visitors a year travel down a long gravel road to see a part of Canadian maritime history. Close by the lighthouse is Wingfield Basin, which is the only safe harbor on the coast between Lions Head and Tobermory. The lighthouse was built in 1896 and manned up until 1988. There is a small house next to the lighthouse that was built in 1958. This house is now occupied by the volunteers from the Friends of Cabot Head Association who live there for weeks at a time during the summer months.

*Time to explore the trails at Cyprus Lake Campground, Bruce Peninsula National Park.*

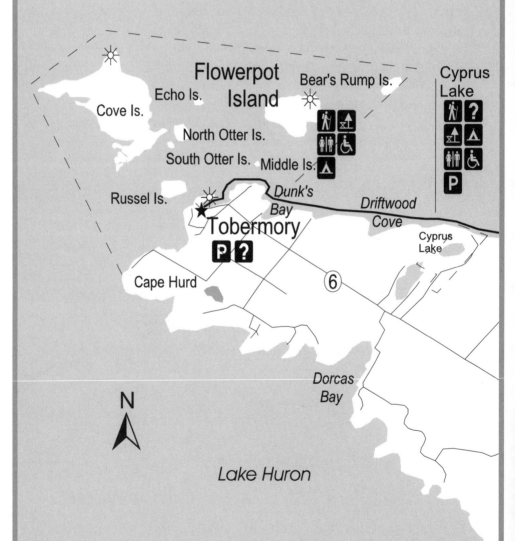

Fathom Five
National Marine Park

Cove Is.

Echo Is.

Flowerpot
Island

Bear's Rump Is.

Cyprus
Lake

North Otter Is.

South Otter Is.  Middle Is.

Russel Is.

Dunk's
Bay

Driftwood
Cove

Tobermory

Cyprus
Lake

Cape Hurd

6

N

Dorcas
Bay

Lake Huron

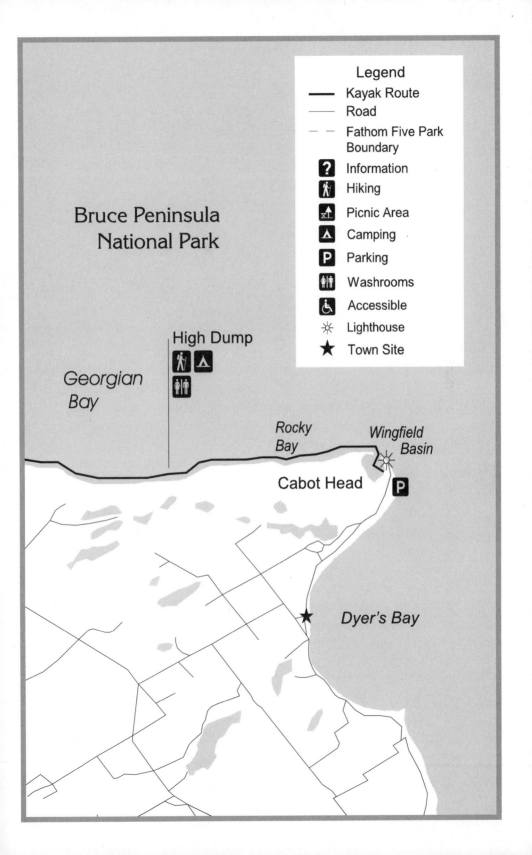

*Lunch stop on the limestone ledges just beyond Cave Point.*

This is an inspiring spot to start a kayak trip. If the weather is slightly windy, you may choose to launch in Wingfield Basin. If it if very windy with high waves, and the weather report does not indicate that the waves will subside, you would be wise not to depart. There is nowhere easy to land at High Dump, the first camping spot. This route is only possible with favorable weather. If the winds are strong and the waves build up, which they tend to do very quickly here, you can be windbound for days. Three-meter waves are quite common, and most of the landing and launching spots are on steep cobblestone beaches. If you are paddling anything other than a plastic kayak, expect to add some scratches to your boat.

All that being said, this is probably one of the most ruggedly beautiful spots on Georgian Bay. If the weather gods smile on you, paddling this route can be a spirit-lifting experience. From Cabot Head you will paddle past tall cliffs, rocky coves and alongside sea caves sculpted out of the rock. From Cabot Head it is necessary to get your vehicle shuttled to Tobermory. If you have two vehicles, you can offload your kayaks at Cabot Head and then, while two people shuttle a vehicle to Tobermory, the others can pack up the kayaks so everything is ready to go once the drivers return. If you are leaving a car at the parking lot, make sure that the volunteers at the lighthouse know and give a good donation to the Friends of Cabot Head for making this access point possible. From the parking area it is necessary to carry the kayaks down a long (300-meter) trail to Wingfield Basin. Half of this walk is on a concrete path between shrubs that are infested with poison ivy. Stay on the path!

The best launch site is just to the left, on a small beach about 100 meters after the concrete path ends. There are plenty of snakes here, so watch your step when carrying your gear to the launch point. We have not seen any poisonous snakes here, though this is home to the Massasauga rattlesnake, but there are plenty of other snakes that are not very shy.

From your launch site, paddle straight across Wingfield Basin and you will see the wreck of the *Gargantua*. This large steam tug has been lying here since 1952, when she was towed into the Basin and allowed to sink. There is a beaver that makes its home within her walls and a small garden of plants and shrubs now grace her upper decks. Much of the above-water structure was destroyed by fire in 1971, but it is still quite an impressive wreck to paddle around. It is also a strong visual reminder of the awesome power of Georgian Bay.

There are two small stone cottages at the entrance to the Basin. These are now owned by the provincial government, but there has been no decision on what they will be used for. Please leave these buildings intact for others to enjoy. As you paddle out through the channel into the waves, the horizon expands in front of you. Look around you; for 180 degrees there is just water and slicing down along the edge of the water are the cliffs of the Niagara Escarpment. The white limestone bottom gives the water a turquoise color that can make you feel as if you are pad-dling in some tropical paradise. As long as you don't go swimming you can maintain this illusion. Once you do decide to brave the water, you may feel as if you are paddling in the high Arctic.

Turn left once out of the Basin and paddle along the shore toward the headland, which is visible in the distance. You will notice that the bottom part of some of these cliffs is yellow and brown and almost perfectly angu-lar. This layer of rock is completely covered further up the coast. These cliffs also pose a problem if the waves are large, because of the reflected waves off the cliff face, which can create very confused and difficult seas to paddle in. This is a danger along this entire coast and thus you must be constantly evaluating the conditions. There are very few places to safely land, so you must think ahead when judging the weather.

The only place to camp on this coast is at High Dump. The name comes from the practice of dumping logs over the edge of the cliffs into the water during the logging era. You will recognize High Dump by the long stone beach and the small blue ribbons on the trees just behind the beach. In the middle of the beach is a clump of cedars that is a favorite relaxing spot for hikers taking a day off on their hike along the Bruce Trail. Be careful of the rocks on this beach. They are quite slippery when wet and have been known to roll over on unsuspecting feet. They will pose more of a problem for those in fiberglass boats than those paddling plastic kayaks. This spot is a wilderness campground within the Bruce Peninsula National Park and as such there is a fee for using it. You are advised to call ahead before you leave on your trip to reserve a site or at least find out how busy it will be. In the months of July and August it can be full, but in the spring and fall it is very rarely completely occupied. There are several tent platforms set within the cedars and there is a composting toilet beside the side trail leading to the top of the cliff and the Bruce Trail. If you have the time, this is perhaps the most beautiful and spectacular section of the entire Bruce Trail. It would make a great day hike from High Dump. Be sure to take lots of water with you since there is little or none available on the trail. All water here should be treated or filtered.

The following day make sure that you get an early start because there is a lot to see between High Dump and Tobermory. As you leave High Dump heading west, there are several points and bluffs along the way, each of which has its own character and personality. Between these points are white stone beaches broken up by huge boulders that have fallen from the overhanging cliffs that tower behind the shoreline. Sometimes the cliff becomes the shoreline and, if the weather is calm enough, it is possible to paddle up to the face and glide along under rock overhang that leans out more than a hundred feet above you. One of the most impressive points along this shore is Cave Point. As the name suggests, there are caves in Cave Point, some at water level, but most at varying heights in the cliff face. In the right conditions it is possible to actually paddle almost into some of these caves, but during even slightly wavy weather it is wise to stay well out from the cliff and the rebound waves that can make this one of the most difficult paddling spots on Georgian Bay.

*You'll feel as if you are flying on the turquoise water. Near Cyprus Lake, Bruce Peninsula National Park.*

Just past Cave Point is Halfway Rock Point, which is a perfect spot for a lunch break. At this place the shoreline is broken by a small bay and the Escarpment here has shrunk so that it is possible to land in relatively calm water. There will likely be other people here since this is an easy hike from the Cyprus Lake Campground at Bruce Peninsula National Park and it is a popular day hike for people camping there. Unlike at High Dump, where any people you saw had expended considerable effort to get there, these visitors have only walked a half hour or so to be there. This area is well worth exploring on foot, and a hike along a section of the Bruce Trail here, or just exploring the rocks around the small bay, is a great way to work out the stiffness in those legs that have been cooped up too long in a kayak. In your explorations be sure to check out the cave with a collapsed section of roof just to the west of the small rocky beach.

About a kilometer's paddle past Halfway Rock Point there is another small bay that is surrounded by high overhanging cliffs. The cliff on the eastern side of the bay has a huge overhanging cap-stone that looks almost surreal because of the immensity of scale. Following this cove is Driftwood Cove, which has a long stone beach curving around in a half circle. It is possible to cut straight across this bay and save yourself some paddling. If you do you will soon round the point into Little Cove (also known as Dave's Bay). At this time the first cottages appear on the shore and you will know that the trip is drawing to a close. It is a short paddle around the point bounding Little Cove on the west to enter into Dunks Bay. Dunks Point is straight across the water, and if the wind has started to pick up, it is possible to avoid the open water in the channel between Georgian Bay and Lake Huron by getting out in Dunks Bay and taking a longer walk back to your car.

If the weather is favorable and you choose to paddle around Dunks Point, be prepared for a sudden change in the wave patterns and height as you enter the passage leading out onto Lake Huron. It is not uncommon for wave heights to double and the wind to increase dramatically once you leave the shelter of the Bruce Peninsula. The shoreline on this last stretch of coast is not backed by the high cliffs you've been seeing, but it is quite rugged just the same. This part of Georgian Bay is called the Graveyard of the Great Lakes because of the large number of ships that have been wrecked here.

The harbor at Tobermory divides into two channels when you enter. The larger channel, Big Tub Harbour, stretches away to the right past the

*The crystal-clear waters of Georgian Bay near Cyprus Lake, Bruce Peninsula National Park.*

*Walkway from Cabot Head Lighthouse to Wingfield Basin.*

*Exploring the caves and rock piles in Rocky Bay.*

old lighthouse. There are several wrecks on the bottom of both Big Tub and Little Tub Harbours. Wreck sites can be identified by the wreck buoys and often by the red flags with a diagonal white stripe that indicate divers below. You will see plenty of scuba-diving activity here because this is one of the best dive sites in Ontario. Fathom Five National Marine Park is overseen out of Tobermory, and the waters in Tobermory Harbour are actually part of the park. One of the focuses of this park is the large number of shipwrecks in the area. The clear water and buoyed dive-sites make this a haven for scuba divers. As a kayaker you have a responsibility to stay clear of any area in which people are diving. If you want to paddle over some wrecks, Big Tub Harbour is not as busy and the water tends to be clearer than in Little Tub Harbour.

The easiest place to land is at the launch ramp right at the end of Little Tub Harbour in downtown Tobermory. Be quick when you are taking your kayaks out at this ramp because it is a very busy spot. From the landing it is a short walk to the car park, and from there you can drive right to your kayak at the harbor.

*Top: Sunken ship* Gargantua *in Wingfield Basin.*
*Below: Looking at Middle Bluff in Rocky Bay on the Bruce Peninsula.*

**ACCESS:**
Cabot Head is north of Dyers Bay on a gravel road. Dyers Bay is reached by traveling on Highway 6 to the Dyers Bay Road cutoff. Follow Dyers Bay Road to the village of Dyers.

**ALTERNATE ACCESS:**
None for this route.

**KAYAK AND GEAR RENTALS:**
G&S Watersports Ltd. Jay and Sue Harris
Box 21, Tobermory, Ontario, N0H 2R0
519-596-2200
Huron Kayak
519-596-2289
E-mail tatour@log.on.ca
www.tobermory.com

**MAPS:**
1:50,000, Topographic Maps, 41 H/3, 41 H/4 & 41 H/5

**FEES:**
There will be a fee for camping at High Dump in 1999. For information and reservations contact Bruce Peninsula National Park, 519-596-2233.

**RADIO STATION FOR MARINE REPORT:**
90.7 FM Parks Canada

**SPECIAL CONSIDERATIONS:**
In the summer months the campground at High Dump can be busy; make a reservation to ensure a campsite.

**DIFFICULTY:**
Advanced. This is wide-open water with nothing to break the wind and very few places to safely land.

**TRIP LENGTH:**
2 to 4 days

**POSSIBLE EXTENSIONS:**
Flowerpot Island and Cove Island.

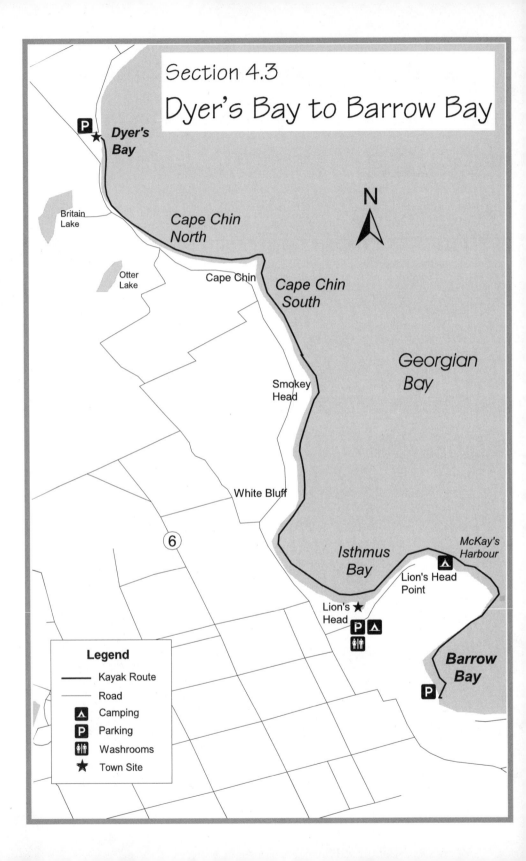

Section 4.3
# Dyer's Bay to Barrow Bay

Dyer's Bay

Britain Lake

Cape Chin North

Otter Lake

Cape Chin

Cape Chin South

N

Georgian Bay

Smokey Head

White Bluff

6

Isthmus Bay

McKay's Harbour

Lion's Head Point

Lion's Head

Barrow Bay

## Legend

| | |
|---|---|
| ▬▬▬ | Kayak Route |
| ─── | Road |
| ▲ | Camping |
| ℙ | Parking |
| 🚻 | Washrooms |
| ★ | Town Site |

# DYERS BAY TO BARROW BAY 4.3

The section of coast stretching from Dyers Bay south to Barrow Bay on the Bruce Peninsula encompasses cliffs, small beaches, turquoise water and a sense of wilderness not found any further south on the Peninsula. We recommend combining comfort with rugged living on this trip. Arrive at Dyers Bay the night before you plan to paddle and stay at one of the many bed-and-breakfast establishments in this quaint little village. You should call ahead for reservations, however, since they can fill up very quickly in the summer. For a small extra fee many of these places will shuttle your vehicle for you to Barrow Bay. It is necessary to have your vehicle shuttled because hitchhiking back to Dyers Bay would be very difficult due to the low volume of traffic actually going into Dyers Bay. Once you have settled in for the night, get your gear ready for an early start the next morning because the weather can be quite change-

*Just south of Devil's Monument on the Bruce Peninsula.*

*Sunrise over McKays Harbour.*

able here and you will want to take advantage of any calm weather that you are blessed with.

The shoreline here in Dyers Bay is a cobblestone beach made up of white limestone cobbles. These can be very slippery when wet, so be careful when landing and launching. It is common to have a small sea of less than one meter running here, so be prepared to launch into small surf. Once launched and paddling south, relax and soak in the surrounding beauty. A half hour's paddle brings you to shoreline that has no cottages and is quite wild. There are high white limestone and dolomite cliffs with white birches around their feet rising from piles of scree. In the fall the colors girdle the cliff in a wreath of gold with green highlights from magnificent white cedars. There are very few maples here so the colors are not as red as they are further south, but they are no less spectacular. The only problem with traveling here in the fall is that the water and air temperatures are significantly lower than in the summer and this leads to higher risks in the chance of an accidental swamping. The weather can be much more violent in the fall as well, but there are fewer people and far fewer boats than at any other time of the paddling season.

Keep your eye out for a staircase made of rough wood leading down from the top of the cliff. Close to this point is a shelter on the Bruce Trail with a stupendous view looking south over the day's paddle. There are very few places to safely land on this shore if the wind blows up large waves, so be very careful when you get in closer to shore. The closer to shore you get the steeper the waves will be and the more risk there is of a capsize. There are many large boulders in the water here that are quite close to the surface, and those of you in fiberglass boats will want to make sure that you don't get dropped on a boulder by a wave.

Just after the first point that you pass south of Dyers Bay, you will see Devils Monument on the edge of cliff. This is a sea stack formation similar to the two on Flowerpot Island. In the middle of summer it can be difficult to see this formation because of the trees growing around it. If it is calm enough to land, it is well worth the short scramble up the rocks to see this natural wonder up close.

As you leave the Devils Monument behind, you will see in front of you a high bluff jutting out into the water. This is Cape Chin, and once you have rounded it the day's destination is in view far to the south. The Lions Head Peninsula juts out into Georgian Bay off the side of the Bruce Peninsula like a large block. It is almost square, and from Cape Chin you can look across the water to the end of the block.

As you paddle south from Cape Chin you will notice a few cottages on the shore but little else to disturb your enjoyment of this area. The water changes from an almost tropical-looking blue-green to a deep blue as the bottom plunges to depths of over 100 meters just off shore. The mix of these colors combined with the white of the rocky shelf and cliff shrouded in a lace of green make this area a visual feast. If you are a photographer, pack an extra couple of rolls of film.

From Cape Chin you will paddle south past white stone beaches to Smokey Head and then on to White Bluff. Just off Smokey Head is a wonderful playground of sunken and half-sunken boulders that makes a great place for a swim if the temperature is right. If you are lucky enough to have a calm day you will enjoy the sensation of flying as you paddle through the crystal-clear waters over boulders and pebbles. The light through the water throws prisms in fantastic shapes all over the bottom. From Smokey Head the shore gently curves toward White Bluff. Behind

*The Lion's Head.*

White Bluff the dolomite cliffs on the Lions Head Peninsula rear up out of the water.

As you round White Bluff you will start to see some cottages again along the shore. You can either paddle all the way into the town of Lions Head or strike across Isthmus Bay toward the cliffs on the Lions Head peninsula. In the summer months and on most weekends in spring and summer you will see rock climbers on these dolomite cliffs. This is reputed to be one of the best rock-climbing areas in Ontario. A kayak provides a wonderful platform from which to watch these human spiders inch their way up these overhanging buttresses. Along the base of this cliff are huge blocks jumbled in piles with a few gigantic ones forming small islands rising straight out of the water. The huge cliffs, large blocks and deep water combine to make those of us traveling in a kayak seem feel very small. It is a truly humbling experience to paddle along under these cliffs.

As you round the end of the cliffs you will see a small indent into the coast with some rock cairns in the trees near the bank. This is not McKays Harbour, which is where you are headed for tonight's camp. Beyond a stretch of shore with many boulders and a flat, raised stone beach there is a small natural harbor with a sandy bit of beach to land at. You may see hikers from the Bruce Trail here since this is one of the camp spots mentioned in the *Bruce Trail Guide Book*. Oftentimes this campsite is a great place to meet interesting folks from around the world and many stories are exchanged while sitting on the beach watching the stars. If you have time, a wonderful way to spend the late afternoon is to hike up to the top of the cliffs, which you were just paddling under along this section of the Bruce Trail. The view from the top encompasses the entire day's paddle and is definitely worth the sweat and energy expended in the climb to the top.

In fact, if you can spend another day out here, this is a great location to use as a base for a loop hike along the edge of the Lion's Head Peninsula. The Bruce Trail follows the coast all the way around and there is a short connecting trail across the base of the peninsula. It is a varied and at times quite strenuous hike, but the view points provide plenty of inspiration to pull you along to the next incredible vista. There is no water at the top of the Escarpment, so take plenty with you when you leave your campsite for the day's hike.

In the morning say goodbye to the new friends that you met the night before and launch off the beach into the waves. It is a short one- to two-

*Playground at half-sunken boulders off of Smokey Head.*

hour paddle into Barrow Bay to your waiting vehicle. On your right will be the towering cliffs running into the village of Barrow Bay and far to your left the cliffs emerge again behind the last few cottages to the south of Barrow Bay. It is possible to land on the cobblestone beach in front of Barrow Bay, but we recommend entering the narrow channel into the lagoon behind the beach and landing in the calm waters inside. Be careful of the zebra mollusks, tiny shells that can shred your hands or feet. They are particularly prevalent near the channel entrance to the sheltered lagoon. Once landed, walk out to collect your car and pack up for the long drive home. If you wish to put off the trip home a little while longer, there is a very interesting artists collective in the old store on the main road in Barrow Bay.